BY THE EDITORS OF CONSUMER GUIDE®

YOUR GUIDE TO
HEALTHY
HOUSEPLANTS

Author:
LARRY HODGSON

Photographer:
CHARLES MARDEN FITCH

Louis Weber, C.E.O.
Publications International, Ltd.
7373 North Cicero Avenue
Lincolnwood, IL 60646

Permission is never granted for commercial purposes.

Manufactured in U.S.A.

8 7 6 5 4 3 2 1

ISBN 1-56173-653-8

Contents

Author:
LARRY HODGSON is editor of *Fleurs, Plantes et Jardins,* a French-language horticulture magazine published in Canada, and was formerly publisher/editor of *House Plant Forum.* His articles have appeared in numerous publications, including *Horticulture, Fine Gardening,* and *Harrowsmith.*

Photographer:
CHARLES MARDEN FITCH is a photographer, horticulturist, and writer, whose books include *Fresh Flowers* and *All About Orchids.* He has also contributed to *The New York Times* and worked with the Brooklyn Botanical Garden and New York Botanical Garden.

HOLMES AIR® is a registered trademark of Holmes Products Corp.

Put More Greenery In Your Life!

Houseplants are a great addition to any home decor.

Scientific studies show that human beings are calmer, more efficient, and more satisfied with their lives when they have living plants around them. Tending to plants is known to be therapeutic, with beneficial effects on both our physical well-being and our mental health. There is also more and more proof that green plants filter common pollutants from the air around us.

Unfortunately, it is not easy to surround ourselves with greenery. Asphalt has replaced green fields and, looking out of our windows, we are more likely to see brick and cement than forests. How can we be sure to have the living plants we need in our highly urbanized world?

One easy solution to this dilemma is to grow plants indoors. Literally millions of houseplants are sold across the country each year. Interior decorators feature them in all rooms of the house, and home decorating magazines never show a finished design without them. Indoor plants are readily available in nurseries, plant stores, supermarkets, and department stores.

Fortunately, growing houseplants indoors isn't difficult. In fact, it can be surprisingly simple. Armed with the knowledge of certain basic techniques, anyone can succeed in growing houseplants. And that's what this book will show you how to do.

Starting with a basic instructional section on how to grow, maintain, and multiply houseplants, you will also find descriptions of over one hundred of the most popular varieties. For faster reference, there is even a chart outlining their day-to-day and long-term care. With all of this easy-to-find information, you will quickly be on the road to success.

Light—
The Key to
Success

Versatile foliage plants grow well in east, west, and even north window locations.

Green plants live off light the way animals live off food: They absorb it and convert its energy into the sugars and starches they need to grow and survive. Without adequate light, no plant can thrive.

Fortunately, plants tell us when they are not getting enough light. Their growth will be pale, and they will stretch toward the nearest light source. Flowering will be weak or totally absent. It becomes impossible to water them adequately: Without sufficient light, they can't use the water we supply, and eventually rot sets in.

The light needs of different plants vary. What may seem like a dark corner to a flowering plant may be perfectly acceptable to a foliage one. Whatever your conditions, as long as enough light to read by exists, certain plants will thrive there.

Window by Window

South Window: This is the sunniest exposure, getting full sun from late morning to mid-afternoon and bright light the rest of the day. Such locations will especially suit flowering plants and those from arid climates, like cacti and succulents. Plants can usually be placed quite a distance back from a south window and still get very good light.

East Window: This location is often considered the best for growing plants. It receives full sun for a short period in the morning and bright light the rest of the day. Cooler than a west window, it allows plants to get the bright light they need without danger of overheating. Both foliage and flowering plants thrive here.

West Window: Like an east window, the west window receives full sun for part of the day and bright light for the rest. Its main disadvantage is that

many plants find such a spot a bit hot for their tastes. Both foliage and flowering plants thrive here.

North Window: Plants in north windows receive no direct sun, but, depending on the season, can receive bright light for much of the day. Generally speaking, only foliage plants will thrive here and even then, they must be grown close to the glass.

Seasonal Differences

Light intensities vary according to season. A south window, which may be too intense for many foliage plants in the summer, is the best location for most plants during the winter months. During the summer, move plants back from hot south or west windows, or draw a sheer curtain between them and the glaring sun. A north window, on the other hand, may not receive enough light for flowering plants during the winter, but almost every plant will thrive in its cool brightness during the summer months. Never hesitate to move plants from site to site according to season.

Improving Natural Light

If your plants show signs of lack of light, you can increase the intensity they receive by removing any obstacles that block the path of the light: for example, curtains, blinds, and outdoor foliage. Even cleaning the windows regularly will help. Another easy way of improving light is to paint nearby walls and furniture in pale shades, so they reflect light rather than absorb it.

Artificial Light

Plants adapt perfectly well to growing under artificial light. Incandescent lamps, however, even those offered for plants, produce light of poor quality that promotes weak, unhealthy growth. They are only good choices for plants receiving some natural light. Fluorescent lights and halogen lamps, on the other hand, produce light so close in quality to sunlight that plants will thrive under them. For best results, use artificial light on timers set at 12- to 14-hour days and make sure the lamp is far enough from the plants so they don't overheat.

5

Watering

How to Tell if Your Plant Needs Water

Plants will often tell you they need water by dramatically collapsing, but it is best not to wait that long, since most plants never recover from severe wilting. Learn to judge your plant's needs by checking it every two or three days.

There are various ways of telling if a plant needs water. Some people go by soil color: The mix changes from dark brown to pale beige as it dries out. This is not always an adequate factor, especially for plants in large pots. The soil at the top of the pot can often be quite dry, while that in the middle is still moist. For that reason, many people prefer sticking a forefinger into the mix. If it feels dry to the touch one inch down, it is time to water. There are moisture meters available that can also test for water needs. Other people prefer to lift the pot. When it approaches dryness, a pot will weigh considerably less. Choose whichever method best suits your needs and stick with it.

M ost plants like their soil kept evenly moist, that is, neither soaking wet nor bone dry. A few prefer that their soil dry out entirely between waterings. No matter what the watering needs of a given plant may be, always water thoroughly, then wait until the plant needs more water before starting again. You can either use tepid water straight from the tap or let water stand overnight. In areas where water is very hard or where water is artificially softened, rainwater is often the best choice for watering your plants.

Above: For people who prefer to water houseplants from above, a long-necked watering can works the best. **Below:** Both plants and capillary mats need to be watered thoroughly from the top the first time. Plants can then absorb water from the moist matting whenever they need it.

Right: Watering plants from below works well as long as you remember to pour out excess water from the saucer after about 20 minutes. **Below:** Wicking is a very effective watering technique for plants that like their soil moist all of the time. It is also a good choice for people who are frequently absent, since wick-watered plants can often go for weeks without being watered.

Watering Basics

Most people prefer to water from above. In that case, water thoroughly until excess moisture runs out of the bottom of the pot. If the plant has dried out entirely, to the point of wilting, this method may not be sufficient, since dry soil often repels water. In that case, set the pot in water until it soaks up all it can hold.

You can also water from below. In that case, fill the saucer with water and wait about 20 minutes. If there is still water in the saucer at that time, pour it out. If there is no water in the saucer, the plant might not have received enough. Add more, come back in 20 minutes, and pour out any excess water.

For plants that like their soil moist at all times, wicking can be a solution. All this requires is a water reservoir (an old margarine container, for example) kept next to the plant and a piece of yarn. Insert one end of the yarn into the top of the potting mix, pushing it down into a drainage hole using a knitting needle. Punch a hole in the lid of the reservoir and insert the other end of the yarn into the reservoir. Water once from the top of the pot to allow water to soak through the wick. From then on, the plant will absorb the water it needs via the wick.

Just keep the reservoir filled with water (or a solution of water and fertilizer) at all times. This method is ideal if you are frequently absent, since wick-watered plants can often go for weeks between waterings.

A capillary mat can also be used. This can be a commercially available capillary mat or a homemade one (old acrylic blankets or pieces of indoor/outdoor carpeting make great mats). Cut the mat to fit the saucer or, for a collection of plants, use a large tray and set the plants directly on the matting. Water thoroughly from the top the first time, then simply keep the mat moist. The plants will be able to absorb water from the matting when they need it.

Humidity

To keep plants looking this healthy, humidity levels and air circulation in the home need to be adequate. Grouping plants together near large windows is an easy way to promote air circulation and increase humidity. It's also very decorative!

Most plants need humid air in order to thrive. That's because the pores through which they breathe lose most of their moisture when the surrounding air is dry, a loss that the plant can't always replace through the water its roots absorb. The thinner the leaf, the greater its need for humidity. Thick, leathery, or waxy leaves, or those covered with hair, are usually relatively immune to dry air. Symptoms of dry air include curled leaves and dry leaf tips, as well as a frequent need for watering. Flower buds are especially susceptible to dry air and may turn brown or simply fall off if humidity is too low.

The humidity level in the average home is often below 30 percent, yet most plants, even desert dwellers such as cacti, prefer humidity levels of at least 40 percent. Many require 60 percent or more. Relative humidity of 50 to 60 percent is probably ideal for both plants and people.

Top right: A room humidifier is a good way to increase air humidity during the winter months. **Below:** Setting plants on a moist gravel tray creates the necessary humidity for healthy growth.

Regional and Seasonal Variations

In some areas of the country, dry air is a chronic problem, especially in the arid Southwest. During periods of extreme heat, air conditioning has a further drying effect on the air. In such areas, the year-round use of a humidifier may be necessary.

In areas with cold winters, humidity levels drop indoors during the heating season. That's because the relative humidity of cold outdoor air drops as it is warmed up. Certain heating systems, such as electric heat, compound the situation by further removing humidity from the air. In such cases, some sort of system to compensate for low humidity may be necessary during the winter months.

Air Circulation

Plants outdoors are exposed to air currents of all sorts, and many seem to need a certain amount of air movement indoors. Air circulation helps ventilate waste gases, remove excess heat, and prevent diseases that can develop in closed spaces. There is often adequate air circulation near large windows because of temperature differences between day and night, but elsewhere, especially under plant lights, it is wise to run a small fan to keep the air in constant movement. Don't direct the fan on the plants. Just having it in the same room will provide the circulation needed.

Top right: Spraying plants with warm water is a popular way of increasing humidity. It's especially effective if the process is repeated several times a day. **Bottom right:** Terrariums are a great way to grow plants that require very high humidity levels. If you cover the terrarium with a glass lid, you can achieve humidity levels of almost 100 percent.

Easy Ways to Increase Humidity

The best-known method of increasing air humidity is spraying plants with warm water. Unfortunately, this is not terribly efficient, since the humidity provided dissipates rapidly. To efficiently raise humidity by spraying, repeat the process several times a day.

A room humidifier will do wonders in increasing air humidity. Just make sure to fill it up regularly. Some modern homes have built-in humidifiers that can be adjusted to the desired level.

It is easy to build a plant humidifier of your own. Simply fill a waterproof tray with stones, gravel, or perlite and pour water over them so that the bottom ones rest in water while the upper ones are dry. Set the plants on one of these pebble trays. They will benefit from the added humidity given off as the water evaporates. By keeping the tray constantly half-filled with water, a nicely humid microclimate will be created.

For plants with moderate humidity needs, grouping them together during the heating season is a simple solution. Each plant gives off humidity through transpiration. Clusters of plants will create very good humidity in the surrounding air.

Terrariums

Delicate, thin-leaved plants require a humidity level of over 70 percent, a level that is hard to achieve in a large room. If this level is impossible to maintain, a terrarium, easily made from an old aquarium, can be the best solution. Fitted with a glass lid, it creates a microclimate in which humidity levels rise to almost 100 percent. Just open it slightly for ventilation if water droplets form.

Temperature

A lmost all house-plants come from tropical and sub-tropical climates with temperatures very much like those in our homes. A daytime temperature range of anywhere from 65° to 75°F (18° to 24°C) is just perfect for them, and most plants have no trouble tolerating occasional summertime highs of up to 90°F (32°C). Generally speaking, indoor temperatures that you find acceptable will also be just fine for healthy plant growth.

Above: Most plants that we grow in our home, such as these geraniums, tolerate indoor temperatures that we find acceptable, including cooler nights and occasional summertime highs of up to 90°F (32°C). **Below:** Some subtropical plants like to be placed near a cool window in the winter, as illustrated by this poinsettia separated from the snowy outdoors by a pane of glass.

Controlling Temperature

Even tropical plants like cooler air at night than during the day. As a result, healthier growth will be seen if temperatures drop 5° to 10°F (3° to 5°C) at night. Night temperatures naturally drop indoors, especially near windows, but you can also turn the thermostat down at night to accentuate the change. Such cooler night temperatures are not only good for plants and humans, they also help conserve energy.

Long periods of extreme heat can be harmful to plants. You can increase ventilation through screened windows or a fan. Air conditioning will also help bring temperatures down to acceptable levels, but plants should not be put directly in the path of cold drafts. Since humidity is removed from the air through air conditioning, some means of increasing humidity may be necessary, especially in dry climates.

Some Like It Cool

Subtropical plants, especially those forced into winter bloom in cool greenhouses, are not as tolerant of warm temperatures as most indoor plants. They can be placed near a cool window in winter or in a room that is only slightly heated. You can also make a mini-greenhouse by bending two clothes hangers into a half circle and attaching them to the window frame, then covering the hangers with a sheet of plastic. Temperatures inside the mini-greenhouse will often be up to 10°F (5°C) cooler than the surrounding air.

Fertilizing

Never try to equate fertilizing with feeding. Plants get their energy from light, not fertilizers. Unless good light levels are supplied and the plant is growing well, fertilizing will do more harm than good. Newly purchased or repotted plants should be given a few months rest from feeding so that they can use up the nutrients already present in their growing mix.

Plants require three major elements for healthy growth: nitrogen (N), phosphorus (P), and potassium (K). These are always listed on fertilizer labels in the form of ratios: 6-12-4, for example, indicates 6 percent nitrogen, 12 percent phosphorus, and 4 percent potassium. Most fertilizers also contain some of the minor elements—magnesium, boron, iron, etc.—that plants also need for growth.

Generally speaking, fertilizers rich in nitrogen (the first number) will

Regular fertilizing is very important for plants that are grown in soilless potting mixes.

stimulate healthy, green growth of foliage, while those rich in phosphorus (the second number) will encourage good root development and improved flowering. Those rich in potassium (the third number) will help build up reserves for plants that have a dormant period.

A fertilizer labeled 30-20-20 would be good for leaf development and would be most recommended for foliage plants, while flowering plants would prefer one richer in phosphorus, such as 15-30-15. Most foliage plants get along fine with an all-purpose or high-nitrogen fertilizer, while one with a high proportion of phosphorus is best for flowering plants.

Right: Slow-release fertilizers only need to be applied once every few months, making them a very practical choice. They are commonly available in a granular form to be mixed with the soil.

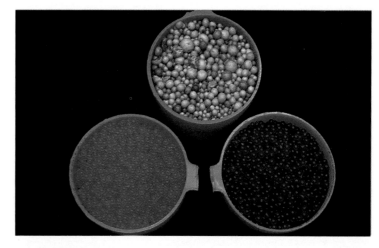

Constant Feed

Most plants these days are grown in soilless potting mixes that offer very little in the way of nutrients, making regular fertilizing very important. One way to make sure your plants get the fertilizer they need is to use a constant feed method.

Simply take a liquid or water-soluble fertilizer designed for a monthly application and reduce its dosage by four. For example, if the label states it should be applied once a month at a rate of one teaspoon per gallon, apply it at every watering at a rate of ¼ teaspoon per gallon. Once a month, take the plant to the sink and leach it carefully by running clear water through its pot until the excess fertilizer runs into the drain. This helps prevent buildup.

Choosing Fertilizers

Ready-to-use liquid fertilizers are convenient, but expensive, since you pay for the water they contain. Water-soluble fertilizers, available in powder or crystal forms, are just as efficient, but are more economical because you add the water yourself.

Some people prefer the practicality of slow-release fertilizers. These are available in granule form to be mixed with the soil or in spikes and tablets that are pushed into the potting mix. They need only be applied once every few months. The label on the fertilizer will suggest a recommended frequency.

Organic versus Chemical

Both organic and chemical fertilizers are available in a wide variety of concentrations. Since chemical fertilizers applied to houseplants do not leach out into the outside environment, even growers who use only organic fertilizers outdoors often have no qualms about using chemical ones on their indoor plants.

One popular organic fertilizer is liquid seaweed. It is applied as a foliar spray and absorbed by the plant's leaves.

Tools

Houseplants do not require a shed full of expensive gardening equipment. In fact, most indoor gardeners find they can get along fine with simple kitchen utensils: a spoon for repotting, a pair of scissors for cutting off yellowing leaves, a sharp knife for taking cuttings, and a recycled window spray bottle for applying pesticides. The most important tool for proper plant care is a good watering can. Look for one with a long but narrow spout.

Potting

Repotting this begonia begins with turning the plant upside down while firmly holding its stem and rootball.

Repot houseplants at least once a year, preferably in the spring. Fast-growing plants may require repotting two or more times a year.

One sign that a plant needs repotting is when it begins to wilt only a few days after a thorough watering. Plants should also be repotted when they threaten to tip over (put these into clay pots or use a heavy potting mix). When a white or yellowish crust begins to build up on the plant's stem and pot rim, indicating an excess of mineral salts, it is also time to repot.

Plants that are difficult or impossible to repot—a tree-sized plant, for example—should be top-dressed annually. This simply means scraping off the top inch of potting mix and replacing it with new mix. This procedure will help remove any toxic mineral salts that have built up.

Right: When repotting, you should choose a clean pot no more than one or two sizes larger than the previous one.
Below: Decorative pots without drainage holes should only be used as outside containers.

How to Repot

Tip the plant upside down, holding its stem and rootball firmly. If it does not slide out on its own, run a knife around the inside of the pot to loosen the rootball. With a pencil or your finger, remove up to one third of the original potting mixture from all around the rootball, gently teasing it loose. Trim off any dead or damaged roots. For repotting, choose a clean pot no more than one or two sizes larger than the previous one. If the plant has reached its full size, don't increase the pot size. Pour enough potting mix into the bottom of the new pot to bring the plant up to its original height. Center it well and fill in the empty space with growing mix. A thorough watering will help the plant adjust to its new home.

Newly repotted plants should be kept out of bright sun for a week or two.

Hydroculture

Plants don't need soil for healthy growth: As long as their roots receive oxygen and moisture, they will thrive. In hydroculture, plants are grown in water using an inert medium such as clay pellets or pebbles as an anchor. A water level indicator tells exactly when to add water, often only once every few weeks. Nutrients are supplied in the form of slow-release pellets or tablets. Although rooted plants can be transferred to hydroculture by thoroughly rinsing their roots of all soil, it is usually easier to start plants from cuttings. Complete hydroculture kits are available for all sizes of plants.

15

Top right: Plant pots come in all shapes and sizes. Plastic pots, for example, are better suited for plants that like their soil kept evenly moist. **Bottom right:** All pots need to have drainage holes so excess water can drain out. **Below:** This jade plant grows best in a soil-based potting mix with extra sand.

The Right Pot for the Job

Plastic pots (and other containers made of nonporous material) dry out slowly and are ideal for plants that like their soil kept evenly moist. Plants preferring drier soil will do better in clay pots, since these allow water to evaporate, reducing the danger of overwatering.

All pots should have drainage holes so excess water can be evacuated. Decorative pots without drainage holes can be used, but only as an outside container.

Potting Mixes

Most houseplants thrive in ready-made all-purpose potting mixes. Most modern mixes are soilless, made of peat moss, vermiculite, and perlite in various proportions. They are light and well aerated, yet hold moisture well, making them ideal for plant growth. Asparagus ferns, caladiums, Boston ferns, and many other plants prefer this potting mix.

Soil-based mixes are heavier and drain more rapidly. They make good choices for cacti and succulents.

Finally, certain indoor plants, such as cattleya orchids and Venus's fly-traps, normally grow on trees in the wild and require very well-aerated mixes. They are often grown in fast-draining mixes such as sphagnum moss, bark chips, or special epiphyte mixes.

Grooming

Simple grooming can mean the difference between an unattractive plant and one that is really stunning, yet it is the most neglected aspect of basic plant care. Here are a few tips on how to turn your ugly duckling into a beautiful swan.

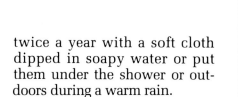

The Quarter Turn

Plants naturally tend to grow toward the light and will soon begin to bend toward the nearest window, causing them to look lopsided or even to topple over. Prevent this by giving the plant a quarter turn each time you water it, so that the plant gets light from all sides. The result will be a symmetrical plant.

Keeping Plants Clean

As plants grow, they produce new leaves and flowers and lose older ones. It is important to remove all dead and yellowing plant parts, not only to improve the plant's appearance, but to prevent the proliferation of insects and diseases that often get their start there. A pair of scissors can be used to snip off dying leaves and flowers and to trim brown leaf tips to a natural-looking point.

To keep dust and grease from building up and slowing growth, clean leaves once or twice a year with a soft cloth dipped in soapy water or put them under the shower or outdoors during a warm rain.

A Pinch in Time

Don't be afraid to prune out unattractive sections of the plant. Generally, for every cut made, two new branches will be produced, making the plant look fuller than ever. Soft new growth can be pinched—squeezed between the thumb and forefinger—to promote branching without leaving a noticeable stub.

A Helping Hand

Plants that are properly pruned and receive a regular quarter turn rarely need staking. However, if an attractive stem has grown to the point where it no longer can support itself, use an unobtrusive stake, such as a section of bamboo, to prop it up. The result will look great.

Top: Pinching soft new growth promotes branching without leaving a noticeable stub. **Bottom:** Removing dead leaves improves a plant's appearance. It also prevents the spread of insects and diseases that often get their start in dead plant parts.

Propagation

Multiplying your own houseplant by stem cuttings is both easy and fun. Just select a healthy section of stem with at least three nodes and cut it cleanly just below the lowest node. Then root the cuttings in water.

Most houseplant enthusiasts enjoy the challenge of multiplying their plants, either to renew them or to have new plants to use as gifts. Not all the methods shown here apply to each houseplant (see individual Plant Profile for specifics), but all can be propagated in one manner or another.

Stem Cuttings

Stem cuttings are the most popular method of plant propagation. The technique can be applied to all plants with noticeable stems. Select a healthy section of stem with at least three nodes (the bumps or rings where a leaf is or was attached) and cut it cleanly with a sharp knife just below the lowest node. Remove any flowers or flower buds as well as any leaves growing from the bottom node. A rooting hormone, available in the form of a powder, gel, or liquid, can be applied to the cut section. While not absolutely necessary, it can help stimulate faster rooting.

Cuttings can be rooted in water, but it is best to use a pasteurized rooting mix such as soilless growing media, vermiculite, sand, or perlite. Fill a pot or other container with mix and moisten it lightly.

Use a pencil to prepare a hole for the stem, then insert the cutting so that at least one node, and preferably two, are covered with mix. Firm the mix, then cover the container with a clear plastic bag to maintain high humidity, which is necessary to keep the young cutting from wilting.

Put the cutting in bright light, but not full sun, and supply warm temperatures. When the plant is well rooted and growing on its own (this can take from two weeks to several months), remove the plastic and treat the cutting like an adult plant.

Once the top section of stem cutting has been removed, the rest of the stem can be cut up into sections and also rooted. Just make sure not to invert stem cuttings. They must be right-side up in order to root.

Cuttings of succulents and cacti should be allowed to heal over before being potted, a process that can take anywhere from several days to more than a month. Don't cover succulents with plastic since high humidity can cause them to rot.

Leaf Cuttings

Only a few plants can be reproduced by leaf cuttings (see individual Plant Profiles), but their ease of propagation makes them very popular plants. Break off a whole leaf, including its stalk, and insert the stalk into the rooting medium as above, covering the container with clear plastic. One or more new plantlets will soon sprout at the leaf's base. They can be potted individually when they are well rooted.

In the case of a few plants (florist's gloxinias, rex begonias, snake plants, and streptocarpus), even a small leaf section can be rooted. Cut a healthy leaf into sections, each one with a major vein, and place each section so its base is just barely covered with mix. New plantlets will soon appear.

Layering

This method applies mainly to plants with trailing stems or to those, like the spider plant, that produce baby plants on stolons. Simply set a pot filled with moist growing mix under a section of stem and pin it down to the mix with a hairpin or twist tie. When the attached section has rooted, cut it free from the mother plant and grow it on its own. Among the plants that can be propagated by this method are hare's foot ferns, episcias, pothos, Boston ferns, and strawberry begonias.

Top: Rooting leaf cuttings works well for begonias. All you have to do is insert a leaf into rooting medium. New plantlets will soon sprout at the leaf's base. **Bottom left:** Propagation by layering is used for plants with trailing stems. **Bottom right:** Stem cuttings are the most popular method of plant propagation. This technique is suitable for any plant with noticeable stems.

Air Layering

The air layering method is used on trees or shrublike plants, often those with thick or woody stems that are hard to root from stem cuttings. Using a sharp knife, make a cut halfway through the main stem, about one third of the way down from the growing tip. Insert a sliver of wood or a match into the cutting to prevent it from healing over. Apply a small amount of rooting compound to the cut, then cover it with a handful of moist sphagnum moss. Wrap the moss in a sheet of plastic and attach the plastic to the stem with twist ties. Check the moss every week or so and add water if it dries out. When roots have formed, pot the new plant in an individual pot and treat it as an adult plant.

Division

Plants that grow in clumps are best propagated by division. Remove the plant from its pot and break the rootball up into sections, each with at least one rooted stem, using a knife if necessary. Plant the divisions in individual pots.

Certain plants produce offsets—baby plants at the base of the mother plant. These can be cut free from the mother plant when they reach about one third of their size. At this point, most are well rooted and can be treated as any newly potted plant. If they are not rooted, treat them as cuttings.

Seed

Almost all houseplants can be grown from seed, although seeds may be hard to come by. It is easiest to buy them from seed companies, but some plants will also produce seeds on their own. Sprinkle the seeds over the surface of a moist growing medium and press lightly. Large seeds should be covered with a thin layer of potting mix. Cover the container with clear plastic or a sheet of glass and place it in a warm, brightly lit spot. When plantlets appear and have formed at least four true leaves, harden them off by gradually removing their protective covering, and pot them individually in small pots. Plants easily propagated by seed are asparagus ferns, begonias, primroses, and parlor palms.

Top: African violets are frequently propagated by division. Rootballs are broken up into sections with at least one rooted stem. Each section is then planted into an individual pot. **Bottom left:** This *Dieffenbachia* is being propagated by air layering. Plastic is used to keep the new cut moist so that roots will form readily. **Bottom right:** Almost all houseplants can be grown from seed. While buying seeds is easier, using seeds from your own seedpods is a lot more fun.

20

Plants as Living Decor

Houseplants are wonderful decorations in any home.

The real value of houseplants lies in their use as decorations for the home. Plants automatically create a sense of coziness and put people at ease. Properly used, they can make large spaces look intimate and magnify small spaces to create an impression of depth. It is hard to imagine a decor that doesn't call for at least a few plants placed in just the right spots.

Movable Plants

The spot in the home or office where a plant looks the best is not always the one in which it grows well, usually due to lack of light. Artificial lights could be installed to improve conditions, but it is far easier to consider plants as movable objects. For every shady spot calling for greenery, buy two plants. While the first plant does duty as a decorative item, place the other in a brightly lit window, then, once a week, switch the plants around. You'll keep your plants healthy and attractive for a much longer time.

Flowering plants need more light than foliage types and can rarely be grown anywhere but directly in front of a window. They can, however, be used as decorative items while in bloom and placed anywhere in the home. When they stop blooming, move them back into the light until they have recuperated enough to bloom again.

Dish Gardens and Terrariums

It is easy to make fascinating miniature gardens in small containers. Just mix small foliage plants and the occasional flowering plant in a decorative dish garden, or create one entirely composed of cacti and succulents. A mixture of trailing and bushy plants, with the occasional upright one for contrast, will create an especially decorative effect. For delicate plants, use glass terrariums instead of trays. If the container is deep enough, don't even unpot the plants—just hide their pots in decorative mulch. Any plant that becomes unattractive can then be easily replaced without upsetting the other plants.

What's Wrong with My Plant?

Most difficulties with plants are not due to disease or insects, but to cultural practices that can be easily corrected. Even if pests are involved, there is an increasingly wide range of biological pesticides, such as insecticidal soap, which can be used around the home without harming its other inhabitants.

SYMPTOM	CAUSE	TREATMENT
CULTURAL PROBLEMS		
Pale growth with new leaves smaller than normal. The plant stretches toward the light.	Insufficient light	Move plants to a brighter spot or closer to the light source. Supply artificial light.
Foliage wilts, potting mix is dry.	Lack of water	Water thoroughly.
Foliage wilts, potting mix is moist. Soil smells of decaying vegetation.	Overwatering	Water less frequently. Increase light so the plant can better absorb the water it is given.
Growth is slow and leaves are pale in color.	Lack of fertilizer	Apply an appropriate fertilizer regularly throughout the growing season.
Growth is stunted and leaves are yellowed. A crustlike accumulation appears at the base of the plant's stem and on the pot rim.	Buildup of mineral salts in the soil	In light cases, leach the soil thoroughly with clear water. In more severe cases, repot into fresh soil.
Plant does not bloom.	Various causes (too little light, too much water, etc.)	Improve growing conditions according to the information given in the "Plant Profiles" section.
INSECTS AND OTHER PESTS		
Leaves take on a mottled appearance and appear dusty underneath. If the leaves are shaken over a sheet of white paper, tiny moving "spiders" can be seen. In severe cases, a spidery webbing stretches between leaves.	Spider mites	Clean plant thoroughly with soapy water. Spray with insecticidal soap. Keep the air humid to prevent a recurrence.
Little balls of "cotton" (actually slow-moving insects or their egg cases) are seen on stems, at leaf axils, or on the plant's root system. Leaves yellow and may become covered with secretions.	Mealybugs	Touch individual insects and egg cases with a cotton swab dipped in rubbing alcohol. Spray the entire plant with a solution composed of 7 parts water and 1 part rubbing alcohol.
Shell- or scalelike bumps are seen on leaves and stems. Plants may yellow or become covered with secretions.	Scale insects	Scrape off the shells with an old toothbrush dipped in soapy water. Treat with insecticidal soap.
Green to black, round-bodied, translucent insects cluster together on new growth. Plants may yellow or become covered with secretions.	Aphids	Wash the plant thoroughly with a damp cloth dipped in soapy water. Treat with insecticidal soap.
Tiny, white, dandrufflike insects rise up when the plant is touched. Small translucent bumps are seen underneath the leaves.	Whiteflies	Use a vacuum to suck up flying adults, then wash the plant thoroughly with a damp cloth dipped in soapy water. Treat with insecticidal soap.

SYMPTOM	CAUSE	TREATMENT
INSECTS AND OTHER PESTS (continued)		
Leaves and foliage are streaked and mottled. Hyphen-sized insects scatter about when the plant is breathed upon. Tiny black excrements are found on infected plant parts.	Thrips	Remove severely infested flowers and foliage. Treat with insecticidal soap.
New growth is distorted and turns brown and dry, eventually ceasing altogether. This problem is very host-specific, affecting mostly African violets, begonias, and cyclamens.	Cyclamen mites	This problem is very difficult to treat. It is often best to get rid of infected plants. An appropriate miticide or repeated insecticidal soap treatments can be used if the plant has great value.
Tiny insects are seen jumping on the soil surface during watering.	Springtails	Springtails are basically harmless. Letting the soil dry out between waterings will discourage them.
Tiny black midges are seen hovering around plants and elsewhere in the house. Grublike larvae are seen in the soil.	Fungus gnats and sand flies	These insects are annoying but relatively harmless to indoor plants. Letting the soil dry out between waterings will discourage them.
DISEASES		
White mold appears on leaves and flowers. Plant parts may yellow and die.	Mildew	Improve air circulation. Don't moisten foliage when watering. Treat with an appropriate fungicide.
Gray, fluffy mold appears on leaves and flowers. Plant parts may yellow and die.	Gray mold (botrytis)	Improve air circulation. Don't moisten foliage when watering. Treat with an appropriate fungicide.
Yellow, brown, or black spots appear on leaf surfaces and may spread until the entire leaf dies.	Leaf spot	Can be caused by various disease organisms. Improve the air circulation around the plant. Don't moisten foliage when watering. Treat with an appropriate fungicide.
Black patches appear at base of stem or underground on the roots. The plant wilts and doesn't recover even when watered. A smell of decaying vegetation may be noticeable.	Root or stem rot	Can be caused by various disease organisms, but is usually linked to overwatering. Start the plant over from cuttings.

Safe Pesticide Use

It is important to use only appropriate pesticides in treating pests and diseases. Read the label carefully to make sure a pesticide is not only suited for the problem you wish to treat, but also to ensure that the product is not harmful to the plant you are treating. Always wear a mask, gloves, and long-sleeved clothing when working with chemical pesticides.

Organic pesticides are the preferred choice in an indoor environment. There are many very efficient organic insecticides and miticides—insecticidal soap, diatomaceous earth, rubbing alcohol, rotenone, pyrethrine, etc.—and powdered sulfur is a good organic fungicide.

Prevention

The vast majority of insect and disease problems can be avoided by using only pasteurized potting mixes and carefully isolating new plants after purchase.

Vacation Care

Plants are living beings and prefer regular care, but frequent or lengthy absences need not stop you from filling your home with greenery. Start by choosing plants listed in the "Plant Profiles" section as being "Very Easy" with "Drench, Let Dry" given as their watering requirement. Some, such as cacti and succulents, can literally go for months without water and should be perfect for even frequent travelers. By using watering systems such as wicks, capillary matting, and hydroculture, described on pages 6-7, you can keep most plants happy for two weeks or even more. The plants that need the least care are those grown in sealed terrariums. They can often go for years without water!

Leaving Plants at Home

If you suddenly find yourself facing a prolonged absence and your plants aren't able to survive on their own, there is no need to panic. There are a few last-minute tricks you can try to keep even difficult plants living during long periods without regular care.

Start by setting them in a shady spot and removing any flowers and buds to reduce the amount of water they need. Although plants normally don't like waterlogged soil, they can put up with it occasionally, so set them in a deep tray and literally flood them with water. After this treatment, most plants can go for at least three weeks on their own.

Top: Fragile plants can be covered in plastic when you are away from home for a long time. Since no water is lost to evaporation, plants can go for over a month without care. **Bottom:** Before leaving on a long trip, flooding plants with water and then placing them on a water-filled tray can keep them happy for three weeks.

If you have especially fragile plants, just water them well and put them inside a sealed drycleaning bag. With no water lost to evaporation, they can go for over a month without further care.

Finally, you can simply leave your plants in the care of a horticulturally experienced neighbor. Have your neighbor come in once or twice a week and water as needed.

PLANT PROFILES

This section features 102 of the most popular houseplants. Each is fully described and illustrated. The following definitions summarize the terms used. For more complete information on any aspect of plant care, see the instructional material at the beginning of the book that starts on page 4.

LIGHT REQUIREMENT:

Full Sun—Intense sunlight with some protection from summer sun.

Bright Light—Bright light with some direct sun.

Filtered Light—Good light at all times, but with little direct sun.

Light Shade—Shady, but bright enough to read by.

WATER REQUIREMENT:

Very Moist—Damp at all times.

Evenly Moist—The soil may dry out on the surface, but never completely.

Drench, Let Dry—Don't water until the rootball is nearly dry.

HUMIDITY:

Very High—Over 60 percent relative humidity.

High—From 40 to 59 percent relative humidity.

Average Home—Less than 40 percent relative humidity.

This dish garden shows off miniature foliage plants well.

TEMPERATURE:

House—Regular indoor temperatures with a 5° to 10°F (3° to 5°C) drop at night during the winter.

Cool—Regular indoor temperatures during the summer; cooler temperatures (55° to 65°F/13° to 18°C) during the winter.

Cold—Cool temperatures year-round, with temperatures down to 45°F (7°C) during the winter.

FERTILIZER:

Balanced—The three figures on the fertilizer label are about equal (e.g., 20-20-20).

High Nitrogen—The first figure on the fertilizer label is higher than the others (e.g., 30-15-15).

High Phosphorus—The second of the three numbers on the fertilizer label is highest (e.g., 15-30-15).

POTTING MIX:

All-Purpose—Standard soilless potting mix.

Cactus—A soil-based potting mix with extra sand.

Epiphyte—An extremely well-drained mix often composed largely of bark chips or sphagnum moss. It may be labeled orchid mix.

DECORATIVE USE:

Floor—Large-size plant.

Hanging Basket—Trailing or climbing plant.

Table—Moderate-size plant.

Terrarium—Small-growing plant that appreciates high humidity.

EASE OF CARE:

Very Easy—Suitable for anyone with basic knowledge of plants.

Easy—Generally easy to grow, but with a few special needs.

Demanding—Has special needs that may be difficult to provide.

Temporary—Best purchased in bloom or fruit, then disposed of.

Aechmea fasciata

Common Names: Vase Plant, Urn Plant, Silver Vase

Light Requirement: Bright Light
Water Requirement: Evenly Moist
Humidity: Average Home
Temperature: House
Fertilizer: Balanced
Potting Mix: Epiphyte
Propagation: Division
Decorative Use: Table
Care Rating: Easy

The vase plant is sold in full bloom, with its bright pink flower stalk rising above its foot-high rosette of silvery, tongue-shaped leaves. The actual blue flowers are short lived, but the flower stalk can last for six months.

Keep the vase of this South American plant filled with water. The mother plant will slowly die after blooming, but not before producing from one to several pups that can be potted on their own. The pups may take four years to reach blooming size.

Agave americana

Common Names: Century Plant, Agave

Light Requirement: Full Sun to Bright Light
Water Requirement: Drench, Let Dry
Humidity: Average Home
Temperature: Cool to House
Fertilizer: Balanced
Potting Mix: Cactus
Propagation: Division, Seed
Decorative Use: Floor, Table
Care Rating: Very Easy

The century plant is remarkable for its large (up to five feet across) rosette of fleshy, gray-green, sharply toothed leaves, each ending in a needlelike spine. Many cultivars are attractively striped in white or yellow. Although the century plant dies after blooming, it can take thirty years or more to reach blooming size. Legend says it blooms only once a century, giving it its common name.

Its size can be kept somewhat restricted by underpotting. Beware of its sharp spines when caring for this plant.

Aglaonema sp.

Common Names: Chinese Evergreen, Painted Drop-Tongue

Light Requirement: Filtered Light to Light Shade
Water Requirement: Evenly Moist
Humidity: Average Home
Temperature: House
Fertilizer: Balanced
Potting Mix: All-Purpose
Propagation: Division, Seed, Stem Cuttings
Decorative Use: Floor, Table
Care Rating: Very Easy

The Chinese evergreen bears pointed, dark green, leathery leaves that are three to five inches wide and up to one foot long. The leaves often have heavy silver marbling. Slow-growing, its thick stems can be cut and rerooted when they grow too tall. Although cultivated as a foliage plant, it occasionally bears greenish, callalike blooms that develop into bright red, long-lasting berries.

The Chinese evergreen is a staple indoor plant, widely used in interior decorating because of its ability to withstand poor conditions.

Aloe barbadense (Aloe vera)

Common Names: Medicine Plant, Burn Plant, True Aloe

Light Requirement: Bright Light to Filtered Light
Water Requirement: Drench, Let Dry
Humidity: Average Home
Temperature: House
Fertilizer: Balanced
Potting Mix: Cactus
Propagation: Division
Decorative Use: Floor, Table
Care Rating: Very Easy

The medicine plant is a succulent with fleshy, gray-green leaves that can grow up to a foot long. The leaves are lightly toothed along the margins and covered with irregular pale splotches. Young plants often have a fan-shaped growth pattern; mature plants take on a rosette form.

The popularity of the medicine plant comes from the sap that can be extracted from its leaves and used to relieve burns, chapping, and other skin irritations.

Anthurium sp.

Common Names: Flamingo Flower, Pigtail Plant, Flamingo Lily

Light Requirement: Bright Light to Filtered Light
Water Requirement: Evenly Moist
Humidity: High
Temperature: House
Fertilizer: Balanced
Potting Mix: All-Purpose, Epiphyte
Propagation: Division
Decorative Use: Floor, Table
Care Rating: Demanding

There are many forms of the flamingo flower, most of which have thick, oblong to heart-shaped leaves on long stalks. Their curious, heart-shaped white, pink, red, or lavender flowers feature a twisted yellow to white spadix (inflorescence) in the center. Each flower can last for several weeks. Under good conditions, flowering occurs year-round. A few species with silver-veined, velvety leaves are also grown for their foliage.

Araucaria heterophylla

Common Name: Norfolk Island Pine

Light Requirement: Bright Light to Filtered Light
Water Requirement: Evenly Moist
Humidity: Average Home
Temperature: Cool
Fertilizer: Balanced
Potting Mix: All-Purpose
Propagation: Stem Cuttings
Decorative Use: Floor
Care Rating: Easy

The Norfolk Island pine, which comes from Norfolk Island near New Zealand, makes an excellent indoor Christmas tree. Its ramrod straight trunk bears tiers of dark green, needled branches much like those of a fir tree.

This plant will eventually reach ceiling height, but since it responds poorly to pruning and is extremely difficult to propagate, it's best to replace it when it grows too tall. It readily drops its lower branches in dry air, low light, or excessive winter heat.

Asparagus sp.

Common Name: Asparagus Fern

Light Requirement: Bright Light to Filtered Light
Water Requirement: Evenly Moist
Humidity: Average Home
Temperature: Cool
Fertilizer: Balanced
Potting Mix: All-Purpose
Propagation: Division, Seed
Decorative Use: Hanging Basket, Table
Care Rating: Easy

Although fernlike in appearance, new shoots of the asparagus fern look just like skinny asparagus shoots. The trailing-to-climbing stems bear numerous tiny, needlelike growths. The occasional white, star-shaped flowers are relatively insignificant, but turn into attractive red to purple berries.

The asparagus fern has the annoying habit of losing its needles if mistreated. Let it soak in water; otherwise it will not get enough moisture. You may need a hatchet to divide its thick, woody roots!

Aspidistra elatior

Common Names: Cast-Iron Plant, Parlor Palm

Light Requirement: Bright Light to Filtered Light
Water Requirement: Drench, Let Dry
Humidity: Average Home
Temperature: House to Cold
Fertilizer: Balanced
Potting Mix: All-Purpose
Propagation: Division
Decorative Use: Floor, Table
Care Rating: Very Easy

The cast-iron plant bears broad, oblong, leathery leaves from creeping rhizomes below soil level. Some varieties are variegated, with cream to white stripes, but lose their coloration if not given good light.

A Victorian favorite, the cast-iron plant is slowly coming back into popularity, but remains expensive because of its slow growth. The common name refers as much to its iron-clad constitution as to the darkness of its leaves: Just about nothing will kill it!

Asplenium nidus

Common Names: Bird's Nest Fern, Spleenwort

Light Requirement: Bright Light to Filtered Light
Water Requirement: Evenly Moist
Humidity: High
Temperature: House
Fertilizer: Balanced
Potting Mix: All-Purpose
Propagation: Seed (spores)
Decorative Use: Table, Terrarium
Care Rating: Demanding

Very unfernlike in appearance, the apple-green, tongue-shaped fronds of the bird's nest fern are whole rather than cut. They are borne from a central, funnel-shaped rosette of fuzzy, brown wool where the emerging fronds resemble bird's eggs, giving the plant its common name. The higher the humidity, the longer the fronds. They rarely reach more than 18 inches in height indoors.

Be careful not to pour water into the rosette or rot may set in. The fronds are easily damaged, so the plant should be placed far from passersby.

Beaucarnea recurvata

Common Names: Ponytail, Elephant Foot, Bottle Palm

Light Requirement: Full Sun to Filtered Light
Water Requirement: Drench, Let Dry
Humidity: Average Home
Temperature: Cool
Fertilizer: Balanced
Potting Mix: Cactus
Propagation: Seed
Decorative Use: Floor, Table
Care Rating: Very Easy

A treelike plant native to Mexico, the ponytail is noted for its swollen trunk and its thick mop of long, straplike leaves that cascade down around the plant.

A veritable camel among houseplants, it can survive for long periods on the water stored in its trunk. Although it prefers full sun, it is surprisingly tolerant of poor light. It is extremely slow-growing, and it is therefore best to purchase a specimen of the desired size.

Begonia sp.

Common Name: Begonia

Light Requirement: Bright Light to Filtered Light
Water Requirement: Drench, Let Dry
Humidity: Average Home
Temperature: House to Cool
Fertilizer: High Phosphorus
Potting Mix: All-Purpose
Propagation: Division, Leaf Cuttings, Seed, Stem Cuttings
Decorative Use: Hanging Basket, Table
Care Rating: Easy

No other genus of houseplants offers as much variety as the begonia. It includes everything from rhizomatous plants grown for their colorful foliage to tuberous plants grown for their beautiful flowers and from compact miniatures to tall shrublike angelwings with silver-marbled leaves. All have asymmetrical leaves, often earlike in shape.

Some varieties go dormant or semi-dormant during certain periods of the year and should be kept cool and dry at that time.

Brassaia actinophylla

Common Names: Schefflera; Octopus Tree, Queensland Umbrella Tree

Light Requirement: Bright Light to Filtered Light
Water Requirement: Drench, Let Dry
Humidity: Average Home
Temperature: House
Fertilizer: Balanced
Potting Mix: All-Purpose
Propagation: Air Layering, Seed
Decorative Use: Floor, Table
Care Rating: Easy

The schefflera is a tree with large, shiny leaflets arranged like the spokes on an umbrella. It is often sold several plants per pot for a fuller look. When a single plant loses its lower leaves through aging, it can look quite barren. When this happens, prune it back severely to stimulate branching.

Spider mites can be a problem if the air is dry. Some of the newer cultivars, such as 'Amate,' are quite resistant to them.

Caladium hortulanum

Common Names: Fancy Leaf Caladium, Elephant's Ears

Light Requirement: Bright Light to Filtered Light
Water Requirement: Evenly Moist (during growing season)
Humidity: High
Temperature: House
Fertilizer: Balanced
Potting Mix: All-Purpose
Propagation: Division
Decorative Use: Table
Care Rating: Demanding

Caladiums are justly popular for their strikingly colorful, arrow-shaped leaves, often so heavily marbled in red, pink, or white that there is little green left. The leaves are paper-thin and easily damaged by dry air. Although it flowers readily, the blooms are not attractive and should be suppressed.

These plants are grown from tubers and go completely dormant after their growing season is over. They should be stored dry in a cool spot until growth begins again, about five months after dormancy begins.

Calathea sp.

Common Names: Peacock Plant, Cathedral Windows, Zebra Plant

Light Requirement: Bright Light to Filtered Light
Water Requirement: Evenly Moist
Humidity: High
Temperature: House
Fertilizer: Balanced
Potting Mix: All-Purpose
Propagation: Division
Decorative Use: Floor, Table
Care Rating: Demanding

Peacock plants are grown for their decorative foliage, often heavily marked in intriguing patterns on the top and colored deep maroon below. Most have oblong leaves rising from clustered rosettes at soil level. Some leaves are attractively waved at the edges. The greenish flowers are of little interest.

The leaves quickly burn along the edges if exposed to dry air, but the plant will usually recuperate if humidity is restored. Smaller-leaved varieties tend to need less humidity.

Calceolaria herbeo-hybrida

Common Names: Pocketbook Plant, Pouch Flower, Slipper Plant

Light Requirement: Bright Light
Water Requirement: Evenly Moist
Humidity: High
Temperature: Cool to Cold
Fertilizer: High Phosphorus
Potting Mix: All-Purpose
Propagation: Seed
Decorative Use: Table
Care Rating: Temporary

The pocketbook plant's clusters of strikingly beautiful flowers are one to two inches across. Each is shaped like a tiny pouch and is brilliantly colored in red, yellow, and orange, often with contrasting spots and blotches.

This plant is generally purchased in bloom or bud and is best discarded after its flowering ceases, since it will not bloom again. To prolong blooming, keep the air cool. It can be raised from seed, but only if cool to cold conditions prevail.

Cattleya sp.

Common Names: Cattleya Orchid, Corsage Orchid

Light Requirement: Bright Light to Full Sun
Water Requirement: Drench, Let Dry
Humidity: High
Temperature: Cool
Fertilizer: High Phosphorus
Potting Mix: Epiphyte
Propagation: Division
Decorative Use: Table
Care Rating: Demanding

The enormous, ruffled, long-lasting flowers of plants in the *Cattleya* tribe are what most people think of when they picture an orchid, since these were long the corsage orchids of commerce. They are available in a vast range of colors and color combinations.

The plants themselves are ugly ducklings, with one or two thick, yellow-green leaves above a wrinkled pseudobulb. They grow in clusters surrounded by numerous aerial roots. Let them go nearly dry during the dormant period that follows their flowering.

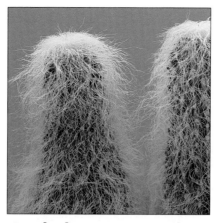

Cephalocereus senilis

Common Name: Old Man Cactus

Light Requirement: Full Sun
Water Requirement: Drench, Let Dry
Humidity: Average Home
Temperature: Cool to Cold
Fertilizer: High Phosphorus
Potting Mix: Cactus
Propagation: Seed, Stem Cuttings
Decorative Use: Table
Care Rating: Easy

This Mexican cactus is so thickly covered with soft-looking white hairs that its columnar stem is often entirely obscured. Don't give in to the temptation of stroking its soft fur, though, as the dense fleece conceals some rather wicked spines. Very slow-growing, it can reach ceiling height, but only after many decades. Flowering is unlikely indoors.

To clean its fur, dip an old toothbrush in soapy water and give it a good shampoo.

Cereus peruvianus

Common Names: Peruvian Apple Cactus, Curiosity Plant

Light Requirement: Full Sun to Filtered Light
Water Requirement: Drench, Let Dry
Humidity: Average Home
Temperature: Cool
Fertilizer: High Phosphorus
Potting Mix: Cactus
Propagation: Seed, Stem Cuttings
Decorative Use: Floor, Table
Care Rating: Easy

The species is a typical columnar cactus with green to blue-green stems and clusters of brown spines rising from cushiony areoles along well-defined ribs. The variety called curiosity plant, which sports bizarre knoblike protuberances, is frequently sold.

The Peruvian apple cactus is often used as a living sculpture in totally inappropriate conditions, surviving for years with no growth and rarely needing any water—then it suddenly rots and dies. In full sun it will grow quite rapidly. The sweetly scented, night-blooming flowers are unfortunately rarely produced indoors.

Ceropegia woodii

Common Names: String of Hearts, Rosary Vine, Hearts Entangled, Hearts-on-a-String

Light Requirement: Bright Light to Full Sun
Water Requirement: Drench, Let Dry
Humidity: Average Home
Temperature: House
Fertilizer: Balanced
Potting Mix: Cactus
Propagation: Division, Layering, Stem Cuttings
Decorative Use: Hanging Basket, Table
Care Rating: Very Easy

A curious plant all around, the string of hearts bears long strings of heart-shaped, inch-long leaves, dark green with silver marbling above and a purple underside. Here and there along the stems are woody, pea-shaped tubers which, if put in contact with soil, will root and produce stems of their own, growing up to three inches in diameter.

The inch-long flowers, while not striking, are certainly odd-looking—they resemble tiny purple lanterns.

Chamaedorea elegans (Neanthe bella)

Common Names: Parlor Palm, Good Luck Palm

Light Requirement: Bright Light to Filtered Light
Water Requirement: Evenly Moist
Humidity: High to Average Home
Temperature: House
Fertilizer: Balanced
Potting Mix: All-Purpose
Propagation: Seed
Decorative Use: Table, Terrarium
Care Rating: Very Easy

Of all indoor palms, the parlor palm is certainly the slowest growing. Small seedlings are frequently sold as terrarium plants and may take years to outgrow their allotted space. A plant only three feet high can be decades old! The plant has a short, green trunk and dark green, slightly arching, fan-shaped leaves. It blooms readily indoors, but the branching flower stems have little decorative effect.

Brown leaf tips and spider mites are frequent problems and usually indicate a need for higher air humidity.

Chlorophytum comosum

Common Names: Spider Plant, Airplane Plant, Ribbon Plant

Light Requirement: Bright Light to Filtered Light
Water Requirement: Evenly Moist
Humidity: Average Home
Temperature: House to Cool
Fertilizer: High Phosphorus
Potting Mix: All-Purpose
Propagation: Division, Layering, Plantlets
Decorative Use: Hanging Basket, Table
Care Rating: Very Easy

The spider plant produces rosettes of arching, grasslike leaves and long, hanging flower stems with insignificant white flowers. Plantlets develop on the hanging stems and give the plant its common names. The most common variety has apple-green leaves striped in white, but there is also an all-green version.

The thick roots of the spider plant quickly fill all available space, rendering efficient watering difficult. It is best to take the plant to the sink to let it soak in water.

Chrysanthemum morifolium

Common Names: Chrysanthemum, Mum, Pompon, Marguerite

Light Requirement: Bright Light to Filtered Light
Water Requirement: Evenly Moist
Humidity: High
Temperature: Cool
Fertilizer: High Phosphorus
Potting Mix: All-Purpose
Propagation: Division, Stem Cuttings
Decorative Use: Table
Care Rating: Temporary

The chrysanthemum is a many-branched plant bearing large, single or double flowers on the end of each stem. The double flowers look like pompons; the single ones like daisies. The color range is vast, including every shade but blue.

Mums are best used as temporary home decorations, to be bought in flower and disposed of afterwards. They can, however, be planted outdoors in climates where winters aren't severe where they will bloom again each fall. To prolong flowering, keep them well watered and at cool temperatures.

Cissus sp.

Common Names: Grape Ivy, Treebine, Kangaroo Vine

Light Requirement: Bright Light to Filtered Light
Water Requirement: Evenly Moist
Humidity: Average Home
Temperature: Cool to House
Fertilizer: Balanced
Potting Mix: All-Purpose
Propagation: Layering, Stem Cuttings
Decorative Use: Hanging Basket, Table
Care Rating: Easy

There is a wide variety of *Cissus* species. Most are climbing plants that clamber up objects by means of tendrils. They generally have shiny, often compound leaves.

They are not especially hard to grow, but they are intolerant of dry soil, losing many leaves if subjected to drought. Don't hesitate to prune these vigorous plants harshly to stimulate branching. Spider mites can be a problem if the air is dry.

X *Citrofortunella mitis (Citrus mitis)*

Common Names: Calamondin Orange, Miniature Orange

Light Requirement: Full Sun to Bright Light
Water Requirement: Drench, Let Dry
Humidity: High
Temperature: House to Cool
Fertilizer: High Phosphorus
Potting Mix: All-Purpose
Propagation: Seed, Stem Cuttings
Decorative Use: Floor, Table
Care Rating: Demanding

A close relative of the true orange, which can also be grown indoors, the calamondin orange is a dwarf shrub with shiny, green, leathery leaves. It bears fragrant, white flowers and tiny, one-inch oranges, often both at the same time. The fruits are edible but so bitter they are usually used only in marmalade. They can remain on the shrub for many months.

The calamondin orange is subject to spider mites in dry air and to mealy bugs and scale at any time.

Clivia miniata

Common Name: Kafir Lily

Light Requirement: Bright Light
Water Requirement: Evenly Moist (summer); Drench, Let Dry (winter)
Humidity: Average Home
Temperature: Cool to Cold
Fertilizer: Balanced
Potting Mix: All-Purpose
Propagation: Division, Seed
Decorative Use: Floor, Table
Care Rating: Easy

The kafir lily is a large plant with thick, leathery, strap-shaped leaves borne from a nearly bulbous base in a fan-shaped growth pattern. It blooms in late winter or spring with bell-shaped, orange to yellow flowers on a tall stalk. It keeps its leaves year-round.

Cool winter temperatures and drier growing conditions are essential. This plant dislikes root disturbance, so pot it into a large pot and only repot every four to five years. Pups can be separated from mother plants during repotting.

Codiaeum variegatum pictum

Common Name: Croton

Light Requirement: Full Sun to Bright Light
Water Requirement: Evenly Moist
Humidity: High
Temperature: House
Fertilizer: Balanced
Potting Mix: All-Purpose
Propagation: Air Layering, Stem Cuttings
Decorative Use: Floor, Table
Care Rating: Demanding

The shiny leaves of the croton are heavily marbled in red, yellow, orange, white, and green, all often on the same plant. The leaf shapes are equally varied: oval, indented, spiraled, etc. The plant makes a magnificent indoor shrub. Fluffy, cream-colored flowers are sometimes produced.

Crotons lose much of their color, even dropping their leaves, if given insufficient light. They are often infested with spider mites if the air is not humid enough. It is best to purchase young specimens; mature specimens suffer serious leaf loss when moved.

Coleus blumei

Common Names: Coleus, Flame Nettle

Light Requirement: Full Sun to Bright Light
Water Requirement: Very Moist
Humidity: High
Temperature: House to Cool
Fertilizer: Balanced
Potting Mix: All-Purpose
Propagation: Seed, Stem Cuttings
Decorative Use: Hanging Basket, Table
Care Rating: Easy

The coleus is a brightly colored shrub with square stems and leaves ranging from heart-shaped to deeply fringed. The foliage can be any combination of yellow, pink, orange, red, or green.

This plant loses much of its beauty when it begins to bloom. The blue flowers should therefore be pinched out as soon as noticed. It is best to start a coleus from stem cuttings each spring. It is also easily grown from seed. Coleus can be grown outdoors in full to semi-shade during the summer.

Cordyline terminalis

Common Names: Ti Plant, Good Luck Plant, Red Dracaena

Light Requirement: Bright Light
Water Requirement: Evenly Moist
Humidity: High
Temperature: House
Fertilizer: Balanced
Potting Mix: All-Purpose
Propagation: Air Layering, Stem Cuttings
Decorative Use: Floor, Table
Care Rating: Demanding

The ti plant bears lance-shaped leaves, usually heavily shaded with red to cream to bright pink, on a canelike woody stem.

This plant is often sold in the form of "canes" at county fairs. These can be rooted and will slowly grow into attractive plants. High air humidity is necessary to discourage leaf drop and spider mites, two very common problems. Even sections of stem without leaves can be rooted.

Crassula argentea (Crassula portulacea)

Common Names: Jade Plant, Chinese Rubber Plant

Light Requirement: Bright Light to Full Sun
Water Requirement: Drench, Let Dry
Humidity: Average Home
Temperature: House to Cool
Fertilizer: Balanced
Potting Mix: Cactus
Propagation: Leaf Cuttings, Stem Cuttings
Decorative Use: Floor, Table
Care Rating: Very Easy

In spite of its name, the Chinese rubber plant comes from southern Africa. It is a many-branched, thick-stemmed succulent with fleshy, spoon-shaped, jade-green leaves that are edged in red in full sun. There are also variegated clones with white to pink striping. Mature plants flower in winter with clusters of pink to white, star-shaped blooms.

The jade plant will survive under very adverse conditions, but its strong upright stems will become weak and weepy in poor light.

Cryptanthus sp.

Common Names: Earth Star, Starfish Plant

Light Requirement: Bright Light
Water Requirement: Drench, Let Dry
Humidity: High
Temperature: House
Fertilizer: High Nitrogen
Potting Mix: All-Purpose
Propagation: Division
Decorative Use: Table, Terrarium
Care Rating: Very Easy

Earth stars bear low-growing rosettes of tough, pointed, prickly edged leaves, often with wavy margins. The leaves are usually strongly patterned, often with both longitudinal stripes and crossbars in everything from muted earth tones to shocking pink. Small, white but rather insignificant flowers are borne in the center of the rosette.

These bromeliads quickly form attractive clusters of plants, and most are small enough for a permanent home in dish gardens and terrariums.

Cycas revoluta

Common Names: Sago Palm, Cycad

Light Requirement: Full Sun to Bright Light
Water Requirement: Drench, Let Dry
Humidity: Average Home
Temperature: House to Cool
Fertilizer: Balanced
Potting Mix: All-Purpose
Propagation: Seed
Decorative Use: Floor, Table
Care Rating: Easy

The sago palm is not a palm, but a primitive relative of coniferous plants. It bears huge, fernlike leaves from two to six feet long, eventually forming a thick trunk composed of rusty colored scales. The leaflets are hard and shiny and look impervious to damage, but are in fact easily bruised. A whole circle of new leaves appears at one time.

Purchase a sago palm of the desired size and height, since it grows extremely slowly.

Cyclamen persicum

Common Name: Florist's Cyclamen

Light Requirement: Bright Light
Water Requirement: Drench, Let Dry
Humidity: Average Home
Temperature: Cool to Cold
Fertilizer: Balanced
Potting Mix: All-Purpose
Propagation: Seed
Decorative Use: Table
Care Rating: Temporary, Demanding

The cyclamen produces heart-shaped leaves marked with silver from a huge tuber only half-buried in its potting mix. The butterfly flowers in white, pink, red, or purple arise on individual stalks from among the leaves.

This plant needs cool temperatures to do well, but will often bloom all winter if conditions suit it. Remove yellowed leaves and flowers by twisting them off. Best considered a temporary plant, it can be rebloomed if allowed to go dormant during the summer months.

Cyperus alternifolius

Common Names: Umbrella Plant, Umbrella Palm

Light Requirement: Full Sun to Filtered Light
Water Requirement: Very Moist
Humidity: High
Temperature: House to Cool
Fertilizer: Balanced
Potting Mix: All-Purpose
Propagation: Division, Stem Cuttings
Decorative Use: Floor, Table
Care Rating: Easy

The umbrella plant bears clusters of green, 18-inch to four-foot stems topped off by green bracts arranged like umbrella spokes. Green flowers quickly fading to brown appear among the bracts.

This is one of the rare indoor plants that likes to be kept soaking wet at all times; it is easily grown in a dish of water. Brown leaf tips will result if it is allowed to dry out. Watch out for spider mites.

Davallia sp.

Common Names: Hare's Foot Fern, Squirrel's Foot Fern, Deer's Foot Fern

Light Requirement: Bright Light to Filtered Light
Water Requirement: Drench, Let Dry
Humidity: Average Home
Temperature: House to Cool
Fertilizer: Balanced
Potting Mix: All-Purpose, Epiphyte
Propagation: Division, Layering
Decorative Use: Hanging Basket, Table
Care Rating: Easy

These ferns are nicknamed by various animal names because of their thick, hairy rhizomes that creep over the potting mix and down the sides of the pot, looking much like animal paws. The fronds are typically fernlike, being roughly triangular and heavily divided.

These plants are remarkable among ferns for their tolerance of dry air. To multiply them, cut off sections of rhizome with at least two fronds and pin them down onto a damp growing medium.

Dieffenbachia sp.

Common Names: Dumb Cane, Mother-in-Law's Tongue

Light Requirement: Bright Light to Light Shade
Water Requirement: Drench, Let Dry
Humidity: Average Home
Temperature: House
Fertilizer: Balanced
Potting Mix: All-Purpose
Propagation: Air Layering, Stem Cuttings
Decorative Use: Floor, Table
Care Rating: Very Easy

The dumb cane is so named because its toxic sap, if ingested, can cause a painful loss of speech. It forms a thick, green, canelike stem topped off by a cluster of large, fleshy, oval to lance-shaped leaves lightly to heavily marbled in white or yellow. The greenish flowers are of little interest.

When the dumb cane becomes too tall, air layer the top of the plant, then cut the stem into three-inch sections, and lay them sideways in a potting mix. They will soon produce new plants.

Dionaea muscipula

Common Name: Venus's Fly-Trap

Light Requirement: Bright Light to Full Sun
Water Requirement: Very Moist (summer); Drench, Let Dry (winter)
Humidity: Very High
Temperature: Cool
Fertilizer: None
Potting Mix: Epiphyte
Propagation: Division, Leaf Cuttings, Seed
Decorative Use: Terrarium
Care Rating: Demanding

The Venus's fly-trap is fascinating because of its curious means of finding nourishment. It has jawlike, red to green traps that snap shut and digest visiting insects. It is a small plant best suited to terrariums.

Give it boglike conditions in summer, but let it nearly dry out in cool conditions during the winter when it will die down to a green bud. Grow it in sphagnum moss. It should be watered with rainwater or distilled water.

Dizygotheca elegantissima

Common Names: False Aralia, Threadleaf Aralia, Finger Aralia

Light Requirement: Bright Light to Light Shade
Water Requirement: Drench, Let Dry
Humidity: High
Temperature: House
Fertilizer: Balanced
Potting Mix: All-Purpose
Propagation: Seed, Stem Cuttings
Decorative Use: Floor, Table
Care Rating: Easy

The false aralia is a small tree producing thin, coppery red to deep green leaflets with toothed edges. They are joined in a finger-like pattern. It can grow to be six or more feet in height. When it reaches this height, its leaves change to their broader, less attractive adult form.

The plant does best in bright light, but many people prefer the way it looks in lower light when it sheds much of its foliage, giving it an airy appearance.

Dracaena sp.

Common Names: Dracaena, Dragon Tree, Corn Plant

Light Requirement: Bright Light to Light Shade
Water Requirement: Drench, Let Dry
Humidity: Average Home
Temperature: House
Fertilizer: Balanced
Potting Mix: All-Purpose
Propagation: Air Layering, Stem Cuttings
Decorative Use: Floor, Table
Care Rating: Very Easy

There are quite a few popular dracaenas, most of which have treelike canes of varying thickness and sword-shaped leaves arching gracefully downward. The corn plant (*D. fragans*) has broad leaves and a thick, woody trunk. The red margined dracaena (*D. marginata*) has much thinner, spiky leaves with narrow, gray, often twisted, canes. *D. deremensis* has shiny, dark green leaves and green canes. All offer variegated cultivars with white, cream, or yellow striping. The flowers are not attractive, but can be highly perfumed.

Echinocactus grusonii

Common Names: Golden Barrel, Barrel Cactus, Mother-in-Law's Cushion

Light Requirement: Full Sun
Water Requirement: Drench, Let Dry
Humidity: Average Home
Temperature: Cold
Fertilizer: High Phosphorus
Potting Mix: Cactus
Propagation: Seed
Decorative Use: Floor, Table
Care Rating: Very Easy

The golden barrel cactus forms a single very round globe of often gigantic dimensions: Specimens four feet in diameter are not unusual. Its ribs are lined with hooked yellow spines. The top of the plant is covered with thick, white wool. The yellow, cup-shaped flowers are rarely produced indoors and, even then, only on mature specimens.

This cactus can tolerate low light for a surprisingly long time, showing no signs of growth and needing almost no water. It will, however, suddenly rot away. For healthy growth, full sun is required.

Epipremnum aureum (Scindapsus aureum)

Common Names: Pothos, Devil's Ivy, Golden Pothos

Light Requirement: Bright Light to Light Shade
Water Requirement: Drench, Let Dry
Humidity: Average Home
Temperature: House
Fertilizer: Balanced
Potting Mix: All-Purpose
Propagation: Layering, Stem Cuttings
Decorative Use: Hanging Basket, Table
Care Rating: Very Easy

The pothos is a common, tough-as-nails plant with vining stems and shiny, heart-shaped leaves that are irregularly marbled with yellow or white. It looks like a variegated heartleaf philodendron. In bright light, its leaves become quite large.

It is often trained up a wooden stake, but should be pinched frequently to maintain its shape. The pothos tolerates shady conditions, but will lose its attractive variegation if the light is too low. Cuttings root readily.

Episcia sp.

Common Names: Episcia, Flame Violet, Carpet Plant

Light Requirement: Bright Light to Filtered Light
Water Requirement: Evenly Moist
Humidity: High
Temperature: House
Fertilizer: High Phosphorus
Potting Mix: All-Purpose
Propagation: Division, Layering, Leaf Cuttings, Stem Cuttings
Decorative Use: Hanging Basket, Table, Terrarium
Care Rating: Easy

The leaves of the episcia are oval and hairy with a metallic sheen. They are available in a range of colors including green, bronze, brown, pink, red, and white. From the central rosette grow a number of creeping or hanging stolons that produce plantlets at regular intervals. The small, trumpet-shaped flowers are usually bright red but can also be pink, yellow, or lavender.

To increase flowering, pinch out some of the stolons. Leaves that roll under indicate a lack of air humidity.

Euphorbia sp.

Common Names: Euphorbia, Spurge

Light Requirement: Bright Light to Full Sun
Water Requirement: Drench, Let Dry
Humidity: Average Home
Temperature: House
Fertilizer: Balanced
Potting Mix: Cactus
Propagation: Stem Cuttings
Decorative Use: Floor, Table
Care Rating: Easy

There is a mind-boggling choice of succulent euphorbias, most of which are spiny plants with thick stems looking a great deal like cacti. The most popular is the crown of thorns (*E. milii*). It is grown for the red, pink, yellow, or white bracts that surround its tiny flowers throughout much of the year. It bears abundant small, green leaves. Most other euphorbias are leafless.

The sap of most euphorbias is somewhat toxic if ingested or put into contact with the eyes.

Euphorbia pulcherrima

Common Names: Poinsettia, Christmas Star, Lobster Plant, Mexican Flame Leaf

Light Requirement: Bright Light to Filtered Light
Water Requirement: Drench, Let Dry
Humidity: Average Home
Temperature: House
Fertilizer: Balanced
Potting Mix: All-Purpose
Propagation: Stem Cuttings
Decorative Use: Table
Care Rating: Demanding

The poinsettia is a branching shrub with milky sap and woody stems ending in colorful red, white, pink, or yellow bracts. It is usually purchased in full bloom at Christmas and is easy to maintain in full coloration until spring.

Getting it to rebloom is not easy. The secret is giving it total darkness for at least 14 hours every day, starting in September, until the bracts start to change color.

Exacum affine

Common Name: Persian Violet

Light Requirement: Bright Light to Filtered Light
Water Requirement: Evenly Moist
Humidity: High
Temperature: House
Fertilizer: Balanced
Potting Mix: All-Purpose
Propagation: Seed, Stem Cuttings
Decorative Use: Table
Care Rating: Temporary

The Persian violet is usually purchased in full bloom with ½-inch blue or white flowers spread evenly over a rounded ball of foliage. The one-inch leaves are shiny and oval in form.

It is easy to keep the Persian violet blooming for three or four months. After that, it begins to go downhill. Although cuttings can be taken at this point, they never seem to equal the original plant in size or floriferousness.

Fatsia japonica

Common Name: Japanese Aralia

Light Requirement: Bright Light to Filtered Light
Water Requirement: Drench, Let Dry
Humidity: High
Temperature: Cool to Cold
Fertilizer: Balanced
Potting Mix: All-Purpose
Propagation: Stem Cuttings
Decorative Use: Floor, Table
Care Rating: Demanding

The Japanese aralia is a fast-growing shrub with broad, hand-shaped, leathery leaves that grow up to 18 inches wide. They can be medium green or variegated with yellow or white.

Excessively warm temperatures in winter, especially in the presence of dry air, can cause serious leaf drop. If this happens, prune severely, leaving the base of the plant bare. Avoid touching newly formed leaves—they can be permanently damaged.

Ficus benjamina

Common Names: Weeping Fig, Benjamina Fig, Tropical Laurel

Light Requirement: Bright Light to Filtered Light
Water Requirement: Drench, Let Dry
Humidity: High
Temperature: House
Fertilizer: Balanced
Potting Mix: All-Purpose
Propagation: Air Layering, Stem Cuttings
Decorative Use: Floor, Table
Care Rating: Demanding

The weeping fig is popular as an indoor tree because its numerous small, pointed, green leaves and gray to beige woody bark fit our image of what a tree should be. There are close relatives, such as the Indian laurel (*F. retusa*) with rounded leaves and the banana-leaved fig (*F. maclellandii* 'Alii') with long, narrow leaves.

This plant tends to lose many leaves when moved. To prevent this, purchase one that has been properly acclimated.

Ficus elastica

Common Name: Rubber Plant

Light Requirement: Full Sun to Bright Light
Water Requirement: Drench, Let Dry
Humidity: Average Home
Temperature: House
Fertilizer: Balanced
Potting Mix: All-Purpose
Propagation: Air Layering, Stem Cuttings
Decorative Use: Floor, Table
Care Rating: Demanding

The rubber plant produces large, oblong, thick, leathery, dark green leaves, often with a red mid-vein. Many cultivars with variegated foliage are available. Although usually seen with a single trunk, the rubber plant can be pinched back and encouraged to branch.

This plant can survive for long periods of time in low light, but it begins to lose its lower leaves. Since these are never replaced, it is better to consider the rubber plant as one requiring high light.

Fittonia verschaffeltii

Common Names: Nerve Plant, Mosaic Plant

Light Requirement: Bright Light to Filtered Light
Water Requirement: Evenly Moist
Humidity: Very High
Temperature: House
Fertilizer: Balanced
Potting Mix: All-Purpose
Propagation: Division, Stem Cuttings
Decorative Use: Table, Terrarium
Care Rating: Demanding

The nerve plant has oval leaves borne in pairs on creeping stems. The leaves are heavily veined in pink or white. The species has leaves up to two inches in length, but miniature versions, with leaves less than half that size, are more popular.

It is best to grow this plant in a terrarium, since it does not like the dry air typical of most homes. Prune this fast-growing plant regularly or start it from stem cuttings.

Fuchsia sp.

Common Names: Fuchsia, Lady's Eardrops

Light Requirement: Full Sun to Bright Light
Water Requirement: Evenly Moist (summer); Drench, Let Dry (winter)
Humidity: Average Home
Temperature: Cool
Fertilizer: High Phosphorus
Potting Mix: All-Purpose
Propagation: Stem Cuttings
Decorative Use: Hanging Basket, Table
Care Rating: Demanding

The fuchsia is a shrub with arching branches and oval, slightly toothed leaves. It has numerous hanging flowers that look like large earrings. They come in various combinations of white, pink, red, and purple, with corollas and sepals of contrasting colors.

Prune back severely in the fall and keep cool to provoke semi-dormancy. It is commonly put outdoors for the summer. White-flies can be a major problem.

Gardenia jasminoides

Common Name: Gardenia

Light Requirement: Bright Light
Water Requirement: Drench, Let Dry
Humidity: High
Temperature: Cool
Fertilizer: High Nitrogen
Potting Mix: All-Purpose
Propagation: Stem Cuttings
Decorative Use: Floor, Table
Care Rating: Temporary, Demanding

The gardenia is a small shrub densely covered with shiny, green, lance-shaped leaves. It is grown specifically for its highly perfumed white flowers, which often fade to cream. They are generally double or semi-double.

Buy this plant in bloom or bud and maintain it as a temporary plant. Even then, it will drop its flowers if conditions are not to its liking. Constantly cool temperatures of about 62°F (17°C) are necessary for new buds to form.

Gasteria sp.

Common Name: Oxtongue

Light Requirement: Bright Light to Filtered Light
Water Requirement: Drench, Let Dry
Humidity: Average Home
Temperature: House to Cool
Fertilizer: Balanced
Potting Mix: Cactus
Propagation: Division
Decorative Use: Table
Care Rating: Very Easy

The oxtongue is a succulent with thick, fleshy, tongue-shaped leaves, often covered with white, wartlike protuberances or white spots or bands. The plants are usually fan-shaped, although some take on a rosette form with age. Tall flower stems bear tubular yellow, pink, or red flowers after a cool winter rest.

This is a particularly easy succulent, not requiring special conditions of any sort in order to thrive and survive neglect.

Gymnocalycium mihanovichii 'Ruby Ball'

Common Names: Ruby Ball Cactus, Rose Plaid Cactus

Light Requirement: Full Sun to Bright Light
Water Requirement: Drench, Let Dry
Humidity: Average Home
Temperature: House to Cool
Fertilizer: High Phosphorus
Potting Mix: Cactus
Propagation: Grafting
Decorative Use: Table
Care Rating: Easy

The ruby ball cactus is a bright red, ball-shaped cactus that grows on a green base. A mutation of a normal cactus, it totally lacks the green pigmentation that allows other plants to absorb solar energy. The only way it can survive is to be grafted on a green cactus that absorbs energy for it. It is generally short-lived. There are also yellow, orange, and bicolor versions of the ruby ball cactus. This plant only produces its pink blossoms under optimum conditions.

Gynura aurantiaca sarmentosa

Common Names: Purple Passion Vine, Velvet Plant

Light Requirement: Bright Light to Filtered Light
Water Requirement: Drench, Let Dry
Humidity: High
Temperature: House to Cool
Fertilizer: Balanced
Potting Mix: All-Purpose
Propagation: Stem Cuttings
Decorative Use: Hanging Basket, Table
Care Rating: Easy

The clambering branches and toothed leaves of the purple passion vine are so completely covered in purple hair that the entire plant takes on a rich, velvety appearance. The orange shaving-brush flowers are unattractive and unpleasantly scented and should be suppressed.

Don't overfeed this plant or give it insufficient light—its attractive purple coloration will fade. It also ages rapidly, so don't hesitate to prune it severely. New plants are readily started from cuttings.

Hedera helix

Common Name: English Ivy

Light Requirement: Bright Light to Filtered Light
Water Requirement: Evenly Moist
Humidity: High
Temperature: Cold to House
Fertilizer: Balanced
Potting Mix: All-Purpose
Propagation: Stem Cuttings
Decorative Use: Hanging Basket, Table, Terrarium
Care Rating: Easy

English ivy is a vining plant with glossy leaves that come in a variety of shades, colors, and forms. Although it is usually grown as a hanging plant, it will also climb up walls or pieces of wood through the aerial roots it produces on its stems. It can also be grown over moss forms to make fascinating "living sculptures."

Modern cultivars usually branch readily, but older ones may need pinching to keep them in shape. Beware of spider mites, especially in dry conditions.

Heptapleurum arboricola

Common Names: Dwarf Schefflera, Umbrella Bush

Light Requirement: Filtered Light to Full Sun
Water Requirement: Drench, Let Dry
Humidity: High
Temperature: House
Fertilizer: Balanced
Potting Mix: All-Purpose
Propagation: Air Layering, Stem Cuttings
Decorative Use: Floor, Table
Care Rating: Very Easy

The dwarf schefflera is not much smaller than the schefflera (*Brassaia actinophylla*), but its leaves are less than half the size of the schefflera's. The dark green leaflets are arranged like the spokes on a wheel around a central leaf stalk. The leaflets are normally rounded or pointed, but some varieties have notched tips. Variegated forms also exist.

Pinch regularly to create a fuller plant, otherwise staking will be necessary. This plant is not as susceptible to spider mites as its large-leafed cousin.

Hibiscus rosa-sinensis

Common Names: Hibiscus, Rose of China

Light Requirement: Full Sun to Bright Light
Water Requirement: Evenly Moist
Humidity: High
Temperature: Cool to House
Fertilizer: High Phosphorus
Potting Mix: All-Purpose
Propagation: Stem Cuttings
Decorative Use: Floor, Table
Care Rating: Demanding

The hibiscus is an attractive indoor shrub with glossy, maple-like leaves and short-lived, hollyhocklike flowers in shades of red, pink, yellow, orange, and white that are over six inches in diameter. Varieties with variegated leaves also exist.

Modern hibiscus are treated with a growth retardant before sale, keeping the plant compact for up to a year or more. After that, the plant will quickly head for the ceiling, although it can be kept under control through regular pruning. Watch out for spider mites.

Hippeastrum sp.

Common Name: Amaryllis

Light Requirement: Bright Light
Water Requirement: Drench, Let Dry
Humidity: Average Home
Temperature: House to Cool
Fertilizer: High Phosphorus
Potting Mix: All-Purpose
Propagation: Division, Seed
Decorative Use: Floor, Table
Care Rating: Easy

The amaryllis grows from a huge bulb and produces a thick flower stalk topped off with four to six trumpet-shaped flowers, often over six inches in diameter, in shades of white, pink, orange, and red. These are followed by strap-shaped leaves.

Bulbs purchased in the fall or early winter will quickly spring into bloom. Cool temperatures at this time will help prolong the show. In early fall, stop watering entirely to force dormancy. After a two-month dormant period, start watering again.

Hoya carnosa

Common Names: Wax Plant, Porcelain Flower, Hoya

Light Requirement: Bright Light to Full Sun
Water Requirement: Drench, Let Dry
Humidity: Average Home
Temperature: House
Fertilizer: High Phosphorus
Potting Mix: All-Purpose
Propagation: Stem Cuttings
Decorative Use: Hanging Basket, Table
Care Rating: Very Easy

Hoyas form a twining plant with succulent, waxy, dark green leaves. The fragrant, starlike flowers, white or pink with a red center, are borne in thick clusters. When they drop, a spur is left behind. This should not be pruned off, since new blooms will appear at the same spot in following years.

Hoyas only begin to bloom when they are well-established in their pots, which may take two or three years. After that, they bloom faithfully each summer.

Hyacinthus orientalis

Common Names: Hyacinth, Dutch Hyacinth

Light Requirement: Full Sun to Bright Light
Water Requirement: Evenly Moist
Humidity: High
Temperature: Cool to Cold
Fertilizer: Balanced
Potting Mix: All-Purpose
Propagation: Division
Decorative Use: Table
Care Rating: Temporary

Hyacinths are renowned for their extremely fragrant, star-shaped flowers in shades of red, pink, white, yellow, or blue that are borne on dense spikes over a cluster of strap-shaped leaves.

If bought in bloom or bud, just put the hyacinth in a cool, sunny spot and keep it moist. Those purchased as bulbs should be potted and put in a cool, dark place for six to ten weeks, then moved into the light. After blooming, the bulbs can be planted in the garden.

Impatiens wallerana

Common Names: Impatience Plant, Patience Plant, Busy Lizzy, Patient Lucy

Light Requirement: Bright Light to Filtered Light
Water Requirement: Evenly Moist
Humidity: High
Temperature: House
Fertilizer: Balanced
Potting Mix: All-Purpose
Propagation: Division
Decorative Use: Hanging Basket, Table
Care Rating: Easy

Impatience plants are bushy with thick, watery stems and pointed, green leaves. The broad, flat flowers have a long spur and come in shades of white, pink, red, and orange, not to mention bicolors. They bloom almost constantly.

Pinch and prune regularly or the plant will need staking. Start new plants when old ones become unattractive. Impatience plants are often grown outside in shady spots during the summer. Watch out for spider mites.

Kalanchoe blossfeldiana

Common Name: Christmas Kalanchoe
Light Requirement: Full Sun to Bright Light
Water Requirement: Drench, Let Dry
Humidity: Average Home
Temperature: House
Fertilizer: Balanced
Potting Mix: Cactus
Propagation: Stem Cuttings
Decorative Use: Table
Care Rating: Temporary, Demanding

The glossy, green, succulent leaves are borne on compact plants that are topped off with thick clusters of red, pink, yellow, or orange flowers. The flowers can last for months.

Christmas kalanchoes are not hard to maintain in bloom, but getting them to bloom again is not easy. In the fall, subject them to 14-hour nights for two months or until flower buds appear. They are often best discarded when blooms fade and purchased in bloom the following year.

Lithops sp.

Common Name: Living Stones
Light Requirement: Full Sun to Bright Light
Water Requirement: Drench, Let Dry
Humidity: Average Home
Temperature: House to Cool
Fertilizer: Not necessary
Potting Mix: Cactus
Propagation: Division, Seed
Decorative Use: Table
Care Rating: Demanding

Living stones are curious plants that almost perfectly mimic the rocks among which they grow. Each plant is made up of only two succulent leaves rising directly from a root system. They range in color from gray to brown to green with varied patterns on top. A solitary, daisylike flower is produced by each leaf pair in late summer.

Water sparingly from spring until flowering; then cease watering altogether until the next growing season. As old leaves shrink in fall and winter, new ones are produced.

Mammillaria sp.

Common Name: Pincushion Cactus
Light Requirement: Full Sun to Bright Light
Water Requirement: Drench, Let Dry
Humidity: Average Home
Temperature: Cool to Cold
Fertilizer: High Phosphorus
Potting Mix: Cactus
Propagation: Division, Seed
Decorative Use: Table
Care Rating: Demanding

The pincushion cactus is a small, ball-shaped to spherical plant that is usually covered in spines or white wool. Some are solitary, but most are clustering. Small flowers in white, pink, or red appear in a ring around the top of the plant and are often followed by elongated red berries.

Total dryness, cool to cold temperatures in winter, and full sun in summer are the secrets to getting this cactus to bloom.

Maranta leuconeura

Common Names: Prayer Plant, Rabbit Tracks

Light Requirement: Bright Light to Filtered Light
Water Requirement: Evenly Moist
Humidity: High
Temperature: House
Fertilizer: Balanced
Potting Mix: All-Purpose
Propagation: Division, Stem Cuttings
Decorative Use: Hanging Basket, Table
Care Rating: Easy

The prayer plant is a spreading plant best known for its habit of folding up its three- by five-inch leaves at night. The leaves are oval and marked with red veins on some varieties, dark spots on others. The pinkish flowers are insignificant.

To avoid brown leaf tips, keep the soil evenly moist, avoid dry air, and leach frequently to avoid mineral salt build-up.

Mimosa pudica

Common Names: Sensitive Plant, Touch-Me-Not, Humbleplant

Light Requirement: Bright Light
Water Requirement: Drench, Let Dry
Humidity: High
Temperature: House
Fertilizer: High Phosphorus
Potting Mix: All-Purpose
Propagation: Seed
Decorative Use: Table
Care Rating: Demanding

The sensitive plant produces thin, wiry, spiny stems and feathery, green leaves. It regularly bears fluffy, ball-shaped, pink flowers. It is grown as a curiosity because its leaves fold up when touched.

Fast-growing, the sensitive plant grows readily from seed and can even be started by young children. It ages poorly and should either be replaced by a new plant after a year or so or pinched regularly to keep it young.

Monstera deliciosa (Philodendron pertusum)

Common Names: Swiss Cheese Plant, Split Leaf Philodendron, Hurricane Plant

Light Requirement: Bright Light to Filtered Light
Water Requirement: Drench, Let Dry
Humidity: High
Temperature: House
Fertilizer: Balanced
Potting Mix: All-Purpose
Propagation: Stem Cuttings
Decorative Use: Floor, Table
Care Rating: Easy

The broad leaves of a mature Swiss cheese plant can measure nearly three feet across. They are perforated with holes and deeply split along the edges. The thick stems bear aerial roots that can be cut off if desired. The plant is a climber and will require some support. In good conditions, callalike flowers are followed by edible fruit.

Although tolerant of low light, plants without at least some sun per day will lose their holes and revert to their juvenile heart-shaped form.

Nephrolepis exaltata 'Bostoniensis'

Common Name: Boston Fern

Light Requirement: Bright Light
Water Requirement: Evenly Moist
Humidity: High
Temperature: House to Cool
Fertilizer: Balanced
Potting Mix: All-Purpose
Propagation: Division, Layering
Decorative Use: Hanging Basket, Table
Care Rating: Easy

The Boston fern bears apple-green, swordlike fronds that arch gracefully down around its pot. It also yields numerous slender, furry runners that produce new plants at their tips. There are many varieties of Boston fern, most with frilly or lacy fronds. Still others are golden in color.

Older fronds turn yellow and should be removed with care so as not to damage the delicate young fronds. The plant looks especially attractive when grown on a pedestal.

Nerium oleander

Common Names: Oleander, Rose Bay

Light Requirement: Full Sun to Bright Light
Water Requirement: Evenly Moist
Humidity: Average Home
Temperature: Cool to Cold
Fertilizer: Balanced
Potting Mix: All-Purpose
Propagation: Stem Cuttings
Decorative Use: Floor, Table
Care Rating: Easy

The oleander's claim to fame is its sweetly scented and abundant phloxlike flowers in red, pink, cream, and white. It produces tall, straight branches up to six feet or more in height with narrow, willowlike leaves.

For best results, put this plant outdoors for the summer. Prune heavily after flowering to keep it at a reasonable size. All parts of this plant are highly toxic if ingested, so keep it out of reach of children and pets.

Notocactus lening-hausii

Common Name: Golden Ball Cactus

Light Requirement: Full Sun
Water Requirement: Drench, Let Dry
Humidity: Average Home
Temperature: Cool to Cold
Fertilizer: High Phosphorus
Potting Mix: Cactus
Propagation: Division, Seed
Decorative Use: Table
Care Rating: Easy

This small, spherical cactus lives up to its name, golden ball cactus, because it is covered with golden yellow spines. As it ages, it eventually becomes columnar. When it is still quite young, it begins to bear two-inch, funnel-shaped, yellow flowers, often three or four at a time, that can hide its crown entirely.

Offsets are occasionally produced and can be used for multiplication. Otherwise it is grown from seed.

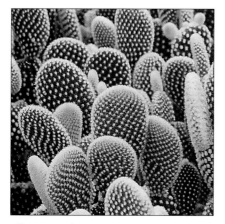

Opuntia sp.

Common Names: Prickly Pear, Bunny Ears, Beaver Tail Cactus

Light Requirement: Full Sun
Water Requirement: Drench, Let Dry
Humidity: Average Home
Temperature: House to Cold
Fertilizer: High Phosphorus
Potting Mix: Cactus
Propagation: Seed, Stem Cuttings
Decorative Use: Floor, Table
Care Rating: Very Easy

Most prickly pears are instantly recognizable as cacti by their flat pads, although some have cylindrical segments. They are often lightly spined, but make up for this apparent lack of self-defense through abundant quantities of innocent-looking tufts of glochids—fishhooklike prickles that break off and stay in the finger. They rarely bloom indoors, but their large yellow, purple, red, or orange flowers are very attractive.

Pads can be broken off and rooted at any time of year.

Oxalis regnellii

Common Name: False Shamrock

Light Requirement: Bright Light to Filtered Light
Water Requirement: Drench, Let Dry
Humidity: High
Temperature: House
Fertilizer: Balanced
Potting Mix: All-Purpose
Propagation: Division
Decorative Use: Table
Care Rating: Very Easy

The false shamrock bears large, cloverlike leaves with perfectly triangular leaflets, green on top and red underneath. They fold down each night and open again each morning. Certain cultivars have bronze to red leaves and silver markings. The white flowers are borne continuously throughout the year.

It is easy to multiply the false shamrock by dividing the numerous scaly bulbs found in the potting mix. Unlike most bulbous plants, it will never go dormant as long as adequate growing conditions are supplied.

Pelargonium hortorum

Common Name: Zonal Geranium

Light Requirement: Full Sun to Bright Light
Water Requirement: Drench, Let Dry
Humidity: Average Home
Temperature: House to Cool
Fertilizer: High Phosphorus
Potting Mix: All-Purpose
Propagation: Stem Cuttings
Decorative Use: Floor, Table
Care Rating: Easy

The zonal geranium is a well-known garden plant that also makes an excellent flowering plant for the home. It bears thick, succulent branches and fragrant, roundish leaves, sometimes marked with a dark, horseshoe-shaped zone. The flowers are borne in rounded heads and come in shades of red, pink, lavender, white, and purple.

Avoid humid air that can cause black stem rot at the base of the plant. Mildew can be prevented by removing faded flowers and leaves.

Peperomia sp.

Common Name: Peperomia

Light Requirement: Bright
Light to Filtered Light
Water Requirement:
Drench, Let Dry
Humidity: High
Temperature: House to Cool
Fertilizer: Balanced
Potting Mix: All-Purpose
Propagation: Division, Leaf
Cuttings, Stem Cuttings
Decorative Use: Table,
Terrarium
Care Rating: Easy

Most peperomias are low-growing, but that is all they have in
common other than their curious,
mousetail flowers. Emerald rip-
ple (*P. caperata*) has heart-
shaped, puckered leaves. Baby
rubber plant (*P. obtusifolia*) has
thick, upright stems and fleshy,
spoon-shaped, often variegated
leaves. The watermelon peperomia (*P. argyreia*) has nearly
round, flat, silver-striped leaves.
And these are only a few of the
many varieties.

Smaller varieties are good choices for dish gardens and open terrariums.

Persea americana

Common Names: Avocado,
Alligator Pear

Light Requirement: Bright
Light
Water Requirement:
Drench, Let Dry
Humidity: High
Temperature: House to Cool
Fertilizer: Balanced
Potting Mix: All-Purpose
Propagation: Seed
Decorative Use: Floor, Table
Care Rating: Demanding

Everyone should try growing an
avocado from seed at least once!
Choose a ripe fruit and carefully
remove the pit. Take off its brown
covering and suspend it over a
glass of water using toothpicks
pushed into its side: Only the
base of the pit should touch
water. When roots appear, trans-
fer it immediately to a good potting mix. When the stem reaches
one foot high, prune it back by
half to stimulate branching.
Pinch regularly to keep the plant
dense and attractive.

Phalaenopsis sp.

Common Name: Moth
Orchid

Light Requirement: Bright
Light to Filtered Light
Water Requirement:
Drench, Let Dry
Humidity: High
Temperature: House
Fertilizer: Balanced
Potting Mix: Epiphyte
Propagation: Plantlets
Decorative Use: Table
Care Rating: Easy

The moth orchid produces alter-
nate wide, fleshy leaves that are
often marbled in silver with no
visible stem. Numerous silvery
aerial roots appear at their base.
The flower stalk is long and arching. It bears up to 30 large, moth-
like flowers in white through
purple, each of which can last a
month or more.

Perhaps the easiest orchid for
beginners, the moth orchid
thrives in ordinary indoor conditions. After blooming, prune the
flower stalk back to just below
the lowest flower, since it will
often bloom again.

Philodendron scandens oxycardium

Common Name: Heartleaf Philodendron

Light Requirement: Bright Light to Light Shade
Water Requirement: Drench, Let Dry
Humidity: Average Home
Temperature: House
Fertilizer: Balanced
Potting Mix: All-Purpose
Propagation: Stem Cuttings
Decorative Use: Hanging Basket, Table
Care Rating: Very Easy

The heartleaf philodendron has long, winding stems that can trail gracefully from a hanging basket or be trained up a support. Its three- to four-inch leaves are dark green and heart-shaped.

The toughest of all houseplants, the heartleaf philodendron can take just about anything other than cold temperatures. This plant is all too often left to take care of itself, resulting in a skimpy look. It is much more attractive when pinched and pruned regularly.

Philodendron selloum

Common Names: Saddle Leaf Philodendron, Tree Philodendron

Light Requirement: Bright Light to Filtered Light
Water Requirement: Drench, Let Dry
Humidity: High
Temperature: House
Fertilizer: Balanced
Potting Mix: All-Purpose
Propagation: Division, Seed, Stem Cuttings
Decorative Use: Floor, Table
Care Rating: Very Easy

The saddle leaf philodendron is a large plant with enormous, shiny, green leaves deeply cut into fingerlike projections. It is one of the tree philodendrons, producing a short, thick trunk and aerial roots to prop itself up. *P. bipinnatifidum* is a close relative with even more deeply incised leaves.

Allow this plant plenty of room: It can reach up to five feet in diameter. If given insufficient light, the leaf stalks will be long and weak, unable to support their own weight.

Pilea sp.

Common Names: Aluminum Plant, Friendship Plant, Panamiga

Light Requirement: Bright Light to Filtered Light
Water Requirement: Drench, Let Dry
Humidity: High
Temperature: House
Fertilizer: Balanced
Potting Mix: All-Purpose
Propagation: Stem Cuttings
Decorative Use: Table, Terrarium
Care Rating: Easy

The aluminum plant is so named because many species have silvery markings on their leaves. They are fast-growing plants with watery stems. Their leaves are often quilted and may be green to gray or bronze in color. There are both creeping and upright forms. Their frothy flowers are too small to be very noticeable.

This plant does not age gracefully, so prune it frequently or start it over occasionally from stem cuttings.

Platycerium bifurcatum

Common Names: Staghorn Fern, Elk's Horn Fern, Elephant Ears

Light Requirement: Bright Light
Water Requirement: Drench, Let Dry
Humidity: High
Temperature: House to Cool
Fertilizer: Balanced
Potting Mix: All-Purpose
Propagation: Division
Decorative Use: Hanging Basket, Table
Care Rating: Easy

The staghorn fern produces two very different types of fronds. The cup-shaped sterile ones at its base are used to grip onto branches in the wild. The fertile fronds are shaped like antlers and are covered with white felt, giving the leaf a silvery appearance.

In cultivation, this plant is usually grown suspended on a piece of wood or in a hanging basket. It is best watered by dunking the entire plant in a pail of tepid water.

Plectranthus australis

Common Name: Swedish Ivy

Light Requirement: Bright Light to Filtered Light
Water Requirement: Evenly Moist
Humidity: High
Temperature: House
Fertilizer: High Nitrogen
Potting Mix: All-Purpose
Propagation: Stem Cuttings
Decorative Use: Hanging Basket, Table
Care Rating: Very Easy

Actually from the Southern Hemisphere, Swedish ivy gets its name from the fact it was first popularized in Sweden. It is a creeping, bushy plant with rounded, leathery, bright green leaves and square stems. Many types have a distinctive odor when touched. Its flowers are of little interest.

Pinch this plant frequently to encourage branching. Old plants readily provide stem cuttings for new plants.

Podocarpus macrophyllus

Common Names: Buddhist Pine, Japanese Yew

Light Requirement: Bright Light to Filtered Light
Water Requirement: Drench, Let Dry
Humidity: Average Home
Temperature: Cool to Cold
Fertilizer: Balanced
Potting Mix: All-Purpose
Propagation: Stem Cuttings
Decorative Use: Floor, Table
Care Rating: Demanding

One of the rare indoor conifers, the Buddhist pine is not a pine at all. It belongs to its own family. It produces long, narrow, leathery, dark green leaves (actually needles) on a woody stem. It makes a nice, if slow-growing, indoor tree.

Often used as a bonsai specimen, it quickly forms an interestingly gnarled trunk when properly pruned. It seems to need cool to cold winter temperatures to do well. It is difficult to root.

Polyscias sp.

Common Name: Aralia

Light Requirement: Bright Light to Filtered Light
Water Requirement: Drench, Let Dry
Humidity: High
Temperature: House
Fertilizer: Balanced
Potting Mix: All-Purpose
Propagation: Stem Cuttings
Decorative Use: Floor, Table
Care Rating: Easy

Aralias are small- to medium-size indoor trees with rounded to deeply cut leaves, often variegated in white or yellow. Most species have twisted, woody stems and branches, making them look like natural bonsais. They are often planted in bonsai pots.

Although relatively easy to grow, aralias have a disconcerting habit of dropping their leaves following any change in conditions. One way to help prevent this is to supply good air humidity at all times.

Primula sp.

Common Name: Primrose

Light Requirement: Bright Light
Water Requirement: Evenly Moist
Humidity: Very High
Temperature: Cool to Cold
Fertilizer: Balanced
Potting Mix: All-Purpose
Propagation: Division, Seed
Decorative Use: Table
Care Rating: Temporary

Primroses are grown for their clusters of abundant flowers in a wide range of colors, often with a contrasting eye. Their leaves are generally hairy and can be tongue-shaped, rounded, or toothed, depending on the species grown.

These plants, of which many quite different types are available, are generally sold in flower or bud and should be discarded after bloom, although some are moderately hardy and can be planted outdoors. Touching them provokes an allergic reaction in some people.

Radermachera sinica

Common Name: China Doll

Light Requirement: Bright Light
Water Requirement: Evenly Moist
Humidity: Average Home
Temperature: House
Fertilizer: Balanced
Potting Mix: All-Purpose
Propagation: Seed, Stem Cuttings
Decorative Use: Floor, Table
Care Rating: Easy

The China doll is a shrubby foliage plant with bright green, hollylike leaves. These are doubly compound, giving them a very feathery appearance.

Before sale, the *Radermachera* is treated with a growth retardant, which causes it to grow normal-size leaves on a short stem. When it wears off, up to a year after purchase, the plant will take on a more open look and will require frequent pinching to maintain its attractively dense growth pattern.

Rhapis excelsa

Common Name: Lady Palm

Light Requirement: Bright Light to Filtered Light
Water Requirement: Drench, Let Dry
Humidity: Average Home
Temperature: House to Cold
Fertilizer: Balanced
Potting Mix: All-Purpose
Propagation: Division, Seed
Decorative Use: Floor, Table
Care Rating: Easy

The lady palm is noted for its dark green, fingerlike leaflets, which look like they have been crimped at the end with pinking shears. It grows in clumps of narrow stems covered with woolly, brown fiber.

This palm should be purchased at the desired size, since it can take years to put on any noticeable growth, although it will eventually reach several feet in height. It is less subject to spider mites than most indoor palms.

Rhododendron sp.

Common Name: Azalea

Light Requirement: Bright Light
Water Requirement: Very Moist
Humidity: High
Temperature: Cool to Cold
Fertilizer: High Phosphorus
Potting Mix: All-Purpose
Propagation: Stem Cuttings
Decorative Use: Floor, Table
Care Rating: Temporary, Demanding

The azaleas sold as potted plants are shrubby plants with small, shiny, egg-shaped leaves on numerous thin branches. During their flowering season, which can last a month or more, each branch is tipped with clusters of white, pink, or red flowers.

Often sold as temporary plants, indoor azaleas can be rebloomed if their special needs—acid soil, cool temperatures, and abundant waterings—are met when in bloom. They are best placed outside for the summer and brought into a cold room when frost threatens.

Saintpaulia ionantha

Common Name: African Violet

Light Requirement: Bright Light
Water Requirement: Evenly Moist
Humidity: Average Home
Temperature: House
Fertilizer: High Phosphorus
Potting Mix: All-Purpose
Propagation: Division, Leaf Cuttings, Stem Cuttings
Decorative Use: Hanging Basket, Table
Care Rating: Easy

The African violet is a low-growing plant producing a symmetrical rosette of dark green, oval, hairy leaves. Its flowers, available in every shade but true red, are clustered in the middle of the rosette. Miniature, trailing, and variegated forms are available.

These violets can bloom almost constantly if given bright light and warm but not excessively hot temperatures. They actually bloom better under fluorescent lights than in a window. Remove suckers as they appear or flowering will diminish.

Sansevieria trifasciata

Common Names: Snake Plant, Mother-in-Law's Tongue, Bowstring Hemp, Devil's Tongue, Good Luck Plant, Lucky Plant

Light Requirement: Light Shade to Full Sun
Water Requirement: Drench, Let Dry
Humidity: Average Home
Temperature: House
Fertilizer: Balanced
Potting Mix: Cactus
Propagation: Division, Leaf Cuttings
Decorative Use: Floor, Table
Care Rating: Very Easy

The snake plant produces thick, pointed, erect leaves up to 18 inches in height. They are dark green with lighter bands. The cultivar 'Laurentii' has a broad, yellow stripe on both leaf margins. In very bright light, the snake plant will produce an erect spike of very fragrant, cream-colored flowers.

This plant is very tolerant of neglect. 'Laurentii' will not produce true from leaf cuttings, only from division.

Saxifraga stolonifera (Saxifraga sarmentosa)

Common Names: Strawberry Begonia, Strawberry Geranium, Beefsteak Geranium, Mother of Thousands

Light Requirement: Bright Light to Filtered Light
Water Requirement: Evenly Moist
Humidity: High
Temperature: House to Cold
Fertilizer: Balanced
Potting Mix: All-Purpose
Propagation: Division, Layering, Stem Cuttings
Decorative Use: Hanging Basket, Table, Terrarium
Care Rating: Easy

The strawberry begonia gets most of its names from the numerous thin, strawberrylike stolons it produces, each tipped with a baby plant. The plant forms a rosette of hairy, round leaves. They are olive-green marbled with silver on top and reddish-purple underneath. Tall spikes of tiny, white flowers are sometimes produced.

Baby plants can simply be cut off and set onto a moist growing medium where they will quickly root and grow.

Schlumbergera X buckleyi (Schlumbergera bridgesii)

Common Names: Christmas Cactus, Holiday Cactus

Light Requirement: Bright Light
Water Requirement: Evenly Moist (spring, summer); Drench, Let Dry (fall, winter)
Humidity: Average Home
Temperature: House to Cool
Fertilizer: High Phosphorus
Potting Mix: All-Purpose
Propagation: Stem Cuttings
Decorative Use: Hanging Basket, Table
Care Rating: Easy

This flat-segmented, spineless plant looks nothing like our image of a cactus, yet it is one. The segments have rounded to toothed margins and bear hanging flowers in red, pink, white, or yellow in fall and winter.

Cool, dry conditions in the fall months coupled with short days stimulate blooming. Moving the plant when its buds are small will cause them to fall off. The Christmas cactus blooms more heavily with time than when first purchased.

Sedum morganianum

Common Names: Burro's Tail, Donkey's Tail

Light Requirement: Full Sun to Bright Light
Water Requirement: Drench, Let Dry
Humidity: Average Home
Temperature: House to Cool
Fertilizer: Balanced
Potting Mix: Cactus
Propagation: Leaf Cuttings, Stem Cuttings
Decorative Use: Hanging Basket, Table
Care Rating: Very Easy

The burro's tail is a hanging plant with long stems covered with overlapping, blue-green, cylindrical leaves, looking much like an animal's tail. The clustered, pink flowers are not common in cultivation.

This plant is extremely fragile and loses leaves when moved. Consequently, it should be left alone. There is a cultivar called the giant burro's tail that doesn't lose its leaves as readily. The fallen leaves root quickly and produce more plants.

Senecio cruentus

Common Name: Cineraria

Light Requirement: Bright Light
Water Requirement: Evenly Moist
Humidity: High
Temperature: Cool to Cold
Fertilizer: Balanced
Potting Mix: All-Purpose
Propagation: Seed
Decorative Use: Table
Care Rating: Temporary

The brightly colored, daisylike flowers that cover the cineraria make it a popular gift plant. The flowers can be white, pink, red, blue, or purple, often with a white ring surrounding a contrasting central disk. The leaves are medium green and roughly arrow-shaped.

The cineraria is usually purchased in full bloom and thrown away when it becomes unattractive. It can be grown from seed but only in a cool room. Watch out for whiteflies and aphids.

Sinningia speciosa

Common Name: Florist's Gloxinia

Light Requirement: Bright Light
Water Requirement: Evenly Moist (growing period); Drench, Let Dry (dormancy)
Humidity: High
Temperature: House
Fertilizer: High Phosphorus
Potting Mix: All-Purpose
Propagation: Leaf Cuttings, Seed, Stem Cuttings
Decorative Use: Table
Care Rating: Temporary, Demanding

The florist's gloxinia is a large plant with a rosette of deep green, hairy, oval leaves and abundant, bell-shaped, velvety flowers in white, red, pink, purple, and various combinations.

This plant is often purchased in bloom, then disposed of, but this is unfortunate, since it is not particularly difficult to rebloom. When the last flowers fade, stop watering to force dormancy. After four to five months of drought, it is ready to start its cycle again. It can also be started from purchased tubers.

Solanum pseudocapsicum

Common Name: Jerusalem Cherry

Light Requirement: Full Sun to Bright Light
Water Requirement: Evenly Moist
Humidity: High
Temperature: Cool
Fertilizer: Balanced
Potting Mix: All-Purpose
Propagation: Seed, Stem Cuttings
Decorative Use: Table
Care Rating: Temporary, Demanding

The Jerusalem cherry is a popular Christmas shrub with thin, pointed, dark-green leaves. The insignificant, star-shaped flowers are followed by round, half-inch fruits that gradually change from green to scarlet.

This plant is often treated as an annual, but it can be kept growing from year to year if given a harsh pruning each spring. Put it outdoors for the summer so insects can pollinate its flowers. The fruits of the Jerusalem cherry are toxic. Watch out for whiteflies.

Soleirolia soleirolii (Helxine soleirolii)

Common Names: Baby Tears, Corsican Curse, Corsican Carpet Plant, Irish Moss, Mind-Your-Own-Business

Light Requirement: Bright Light to Filtered Light
Water Requirement: Very Moist
Humidity: Very High
Temperature: House to Cool
Fertilizer: Balanced
Potting Mix: All-Purpose
Propagation: Division, Stem Cuttings
Decorative Use: Table, Terrarium
Care Rating: Demanding

Baby tears is a mosslike, creeping plant composed of threadlike stems with tiny, kidney-shaped, apple-green leaves. It attractively drapes itself over the side of the pot or, if pinched, makes a perfect mound of foliage.

Although it likes high humidity, baby tears also needs good air circulation. That is why it will not do well in covered terrariums. A piece of stem pressed onto damp mix will soon root.

Spathiphyllum sp.

Common Names: Peace Lily, Spathe Flower

Light Requirement: Light Shade to Filtered Light
Water Requirement: Evenly Moist
Humidity: Average Home
Temperature: House
Fertilizer: Balanced
Potting Mix: All-Purpose
Propagation: Division
Decorative Use: Floor, Table
Care Rating: Very Easy

The peace lily features oblong, leathery leaves that arch out from the plant's base. White "flowers" (actually a colored leaf surrounding a club-shaped flower cluster) rise above the foliage throughout the year. It is excellent in locations with low light intensity.

Overall, this is one of the easiest of all the flowering plants. It will bloom in shade, but flowers more abundantly with filtered light, and it is attractive even when not in bloom.

Streptocarpus hybridus

Common Names: Strepto-carpus, Cape Primrose

Light Requirement: Bright Light
Water Requirement: Drench, Let Dry
Humidity: High
Temperature: House to Cool
Fertilizer: High Phosphorus
Potting Mix: All-Purpose
Propagation: Division, Leaf Cuttings, Seed
Decorative Use: Table
Care Rating: Demanding

The streptocarpus is a stemless plant with curiously textured, long, thick, tongue-shaped leaves. Flower stalks bearing white, pink, blue, purple, or red trumpet-shaped flowers, often with contrasting veining, are borne directly from the leaf.

This plant dislikes summer heat and should be moved to a cool spot, like a basement, at that time. Flowering will occur almost constantly when the plant is happy. When an older leaf shows no more flower buds at its base, remove it.

Syngonium podophyllum (Nephthytis)

Common Names: Arrow-head Vine, Arrowhead Plant

Light Requirement: Bright Light to Light Shade
Water Requirement: Drench, Let Dry
Humidity: High
Temperature: House
Fertilizer: Balanced
Potting Mix: All-Purpose
Propagation: Stem Cuttings
Decorative Use: Floor, Hanging Basket, Table
Care Rating: Very Easy

Young arrowhead vines have upward-growing stems and arrow-shaped leaves. As they age, they take on a climbing habit, and the leaves slowly become multilobed. Many varieties have white, silver, or pink markings on the upper leaf surface.

This plant is as easy to grow as a heartleaf philodendron, which it resembles in its adult phase. It can be trained up a moss form to make an attractive floor plant or allowed to cascade from a hanging basket.

Tillandsia sp.

Common Name: Air Plant

Light Requirement: Bright Light
Water Requirement: Drench, Let Dry
Humidity: High
Temperature: House
Fertilizer: High Phosphorus
Potting Mix: Epiphyte
Propagation: Division, Seed
Decorative Use: Hanging Basket, Table
Care Rating: Easy

There is a wide variety of air plants, most being small, rosette-forming, grasslike plants with green to silvery leaves. The whole plant often turns fiery red at flowering time, producing clusters of flowers in contrasting colors.

Air plants have little or no root system and are generally grown on pieces of wood or decorative shells. To water them, dip the entire plant in water once a week. Offsets can be glued onto new supports.

Tolmiea menziesii

Common Names: Piggyback Plant, Mother of Thousands, Youth-on-Age

Light Requirement: Bright Light to Filtered Light
Water Requirement: Evenly Moist
Humidity: Average Home
Temperature: Cool to Cold
Fertilizer: Balanced
Potting Mix: All-Purpose
Propagation: Division, Layering, Leaf Cuttings
Decorative Use: Hanging Basket, Table
Care Rating: Easy

The piggyback plant bears long-stalked, hairy, heart-shaped, apple-green leaves with toothed margins. A baby plant is produced from the center of each leaf and, as it grows, its weight causes the leaf to trail. A variegated version is also common.

This plant is not hard to grow if good air circulation can be provided during periods of extreme heat. Baby plants cut off and pressed onto the surface of a moist potting mix will quickly grow to adult size.

Tradescantia sp.

Common Names: Spider-wort, Inch Plant, Wandering Jew

Light Requirement: Bright Light to Filtered Light
Water Requirement: Evenly Moist
Humidity: Average Home
Temperature: House
Fertilizer: Balanced
Potting Mix: All-Purpose
Propagation: Layering, Stem Cuttings
Decorative Use: Hanging Basket, Table
Care Rating: Very Easy

There are many different kinds of spiderworts, some with smooth leaves, others with hairy ones. All have trailing stems. Many are striped in white or white and pink. All have stalkless, pointed leaves. Some varieties produce white to bright pink flowers.

Spiderworts tend to lose their lower leaves as they age and should be pruned regularly or started from cuttings. Fast-growing, they can be grown from cutting to adult plant in only a few months.

Zebrina pendula

Common Name: Wandering Jew

Light Requirement: Bright Light to Filtered Light
Water Requirement: Drench, Let Dry
Humidity: Average Home
Temperature: House
Fertilizer: Balanced
Potting Mix: All-Purpose
Propagation: Layering, Stem Cuttings
Decorative Use: Hanging Basket, Table
Care Rating: Very Easy

The wandering Jew looks very much like its close cousin, the spiderwort, and shows this relationship through its trailing stems and stalkless, pointed leaves. The leaves, about two inches long, are shiny, with two silver stripes on the upper surface and a rich purple underside. There are also variegated versions with bronze, pink, or cream stripes.

Prune wandering Jews heavily to keep them young or start new plants from cuttings. Their stems sometimes "escape" and end up as ground covers in other pots.

PLANT CARE CHART

Plant columns (left to right):
1. *Aechmea fasciata* (Vase Plant)
2. *Agave americana* (Century Plant)
3. *Aglaonema* sp. (Chinese Evergreen)
4. *Aloe barbadense* (Medicine Plant)
5. *Anthurium* sp. (Flamingo Flower)
6. *Araucaria heterophylla* (Norfolk Island Pine)
7. *Asparagus* sp. (Asparagus Fern)
8. *Aspidistra elatior* (Cast-Iron Plant)
9. *Asplenium nidus* (Bird's Nest Fern)
10. *Beaucarnea recurvata* (Ponytail)
11. *Begonia* sp. (Begonia)
12. *Brassaia actinophylla* (Schefflera)
13. *Caladium hortulanum* (Fancy Leaf Caladium)
14. *Calathea* sp. (Peacock Plant)
15. *Calceolaria herbeohybrida* (Pocketbook Plant)
16. *Cattleya* sp. (Cattleya Orchid)
17. *Cephalocereus senilis* (Old Man Cactus)
18. *Cereus peruvianus* (Peruvian Apple Cactus)
19. *Ceropegia woodii* (String of Hearts)
20. *Chamaedorea elegans* (Parlor Palm)
21. *Chlorophytum comosum* (Spider Plant)
22. *Chrysanthemum morifolium* (Chrysanthemum)
23. *Cissus* sp. (Grape Ivy)
24. *X Citrofortunella mitis* (Calamondin Orange)

Category	Attribute	1	2	3	4	5	6	7	8	9	10	11	12	13	14	15	16	17	18	19	20	21	22	23	24
Light Requirement	Full Sun		■								■						■	■	■	■					■
	Bright Light	■	■		■	■	■	■	■	■	■	■	■	■	■	■	■		■	■	■	■	■	■	■
	Filtered Light			■	■	■	■	■	■	■	■	■	■	■			■				■	■	■	■	
	Light Shade			■																					
Water Requirement	Very Moist																								
	Evenly Moist	■		■		■	■	■		■				■	■	■					■	■	■	■	
	Drench, Let Dry		■		■				■		■	■	■				■	■	■	■					■
Humidity	Very High																								
	High					■			■					■	■	■	■				■			■	■
	Average Home	■	■	■	■		■	■	■		■	■	■				■		■		■	■		■	
Temperature	House	■	■	■	■	■			■	■			■	■	■						■	■		■	■
	Cool		■				■	■	■	■		■	■			■	■	■	■		■	■	■	■	
	Cold									■						■		■							
Fertilizer	Balanced	■	■	■	■	■	■	■	■	■		■	■	■						■	■			■	
	High Nitrogen																								
	High Phosphorus										■					■	■	■	■			■	■		■
Type of Potting Mix	All-Purpose			■		■	■	■	■	■		■	■	■	■	■					■	■	■	■	■
	Cactus		■		■						■							■	■	■					
	Epiphyte	■				■											■								
Propagation	Air Layering												■												
	Division	■	■	■	■	■		■	■			■		■	■		■			■	■		■	■	
	Layering																			■	■			■	
	Leaf Cuttings											■													
	Seed		■	■				■		■	■	■	■				■		■	■		■			■
	Stem Cuttings			■			■					■							■	■			■	■	■
Decorative Use	Hanging Basket							■					■							■		■		■	
	Floor Plant		■	■	■	■	■		■			■			■				■						■
	Table Plant	■	■	■	■	■		■	■	■		■	■	■	■	■	■	■	■	■	■	■	■	■	■
	Terrarium Plant									■												■			
Care Rating	Very Easy		■	■	■				■	■										■	■	■			
	Easy	■				■		■				■	■						■	■				■	
	Demanding				■					■					■	■	■								■
	Temporary															■							■		
Other Traits	Attractive Flowers	■				■						■					■	■		■				■	■
	Climbing or Trailing							■					■							■		■		■	
	Colorful Foliage	■	■	■	■							■		■	■					■		■			
	Decorative Fruit			■				■																	■
	Fragrance																								■

60

Column headers (left to right):

- *Clivia miniata* (Kafir Lily)
- *Codiaeum variegatum pictum* (Croton)
- *Coleus blumei* (Coleus)
- *Cordyline terminalis* (Ti Plant)
- *Crassula argentea* (Jade Plant)
- *Cryptanthus* sp. (Earth Star)
- *Cycas revoluta* (Sago Palm)
- *Cyclamen persicum* (Florist's Cyclamen)
- *Cyperus alternifolius* (Umbrella Plant)
- *Davallia* sp. (Hare's Foot Fern)
- *Dieffenbachia* sp. (Dumb Cane)
- *Dionaea muscipula* (Venus's Fly-Trap)
- *Dizygotheca elegantissima* (False Aralia)
- *Dracaena* sp. (Dracaena)
- *Echinocactus grusonii* (Golden Barrel)
- *Epipremnum aureum* (Pothos)
- *Episcia* sp. (Episcia)
- *Euphorbia* sp. (Euphorbia)
- *Euphorbia pulcherrima* (Poinsettia)
- *Exacum affine* (Persian Violet)
- *Fatsia japonica* (Japanese Aralia)
- *Ficus benjamina* (Weeping Fig)
- *Ficus elastica* (Rubber Plant)
- *Fittonia verschaffeltii* (Nerve Plant)
- *Fuchsia* sp. (Fuchsia)
- *Gardenia jasminoides* (Gardenia)
- *Gasteria* sp. (Oxtongue)
- *Gymnocalycium mihanovichii* 'Ruby Ball' (Ruby Ball Cactus)
- *Gynura aurantiaca sarmentosa* (Purple Passion Vine)
- *Hedera helix* (English Ivy)
- *Heptapleurum arboricola* (Dwarf Schefflera)
- *Hibiscus rosa-sinensis* (Hibiscus)
- *Hippeastrum* sp. (Amaryllis)
- *Hoya carnosa* (Wax Plant)
- *Hyacinthus orientalis* (Hyacinth)
- *Impatiens wallerana* (Impatience Plant)

61

		Kalanchoe blossfeldiana (Christmas Kalanchoe)	Lithops sp. (Living Stones)	Mammillaria sp. (Pincushion Cactus)	Maranta leuconeura (Prayer Plant)	Mimosa pudica (Sensitive Plant)	Monstera deliciosa (Swiss Cheese Plant)	Nephrolepis exaltata 'Bostoniensis' (Boston Fern)	Nerium oleander (Oleander)	Notocactus leninghausii (Golden Ball Cactus)	Opuntia sp. (Prickly Pear)	Oxalis regnellii (False Shamrock)	Pelargonium hortorum (Zonal Geranium)	Peperomia sp. (Peperomia)	Persea americana (Avocado)	Phalaenopsis sp. (Moth Orchid)	Philodendron scandens oxycardium (Heartleaf Philodendron)	Philodendron selloum (Saddle Leaf Philodendron)	Pilea sp. (Aluminum Plant)	Platycerium bifurcatum (Staghorn Fern)	Plectranthus australis (Swedish Ivy)	Podocarpus macrophyllus (Buddhist Pine)	Polyscias sp. (Aralia)	Primula sp. (Primrose)
Light Requirement	Full Sun	■	■	■					■	■	■		■											
	Bright Light	■	■	■	■	■	■	■	■	■			■	■	■	■	■	■	■	■	■	■	■	■
	Filtered Light				■		■						■		■	■	■	■			■	■	■	
	Light Shade																			■				
Water Requirement	Very Moist																							
	Evenly Moist				■			■	■												■			■
	Drench, Let Dry	■	■	■		■	■			■	■	■	■	■	■	■	■	■	■	■		■	■	
Humidity	Very High																							■
	High				■	■	■	■					■			■	■	■	■	■	■		■	
	Average Home	■	■	■					■	■	■		■					■				■		
Temperature	House	■	■		■	■	■		■			■	■	■	■	■	■	■	■	■	■		■	
	Cool		■	■				■	■	■	■	■	■	■						■		■		■
	Cold		■						■	■	■											■		■
Fertilizer	Balanced	■				■		■	■			■		■	■	■	■	■	■		■	■	■	■
	High Nitrogen																			■				
	High Phosphorus			■		■				■	■													
Type of Potting Mix	All-Purpose				■	■	■	■	■			■	■	■	■	■		■	■	■	■	■	■	■
	Cactus	■	■	■						■	■													
	Epiphyte																■							
Propagation	Air Layering																							
	Division		■	■	■			■		■			■					■		■				■
	Layering						■																	
	Leaf Cuttings														■									
	Seed		■	■		■				■	■					■			■					■
	Stem Cuttings	■			■		■		■		■		■	■			■	■	■		■	■	■	
Decorative Use	Hanging Basket				■			■										■			■	■		
	Floor Plant						■		■		■		■		■			■				■	■	
	Table Plant	■	■	■	■	■	■	■	■			■	■	■	■	■	■	■	■		■	■	■	■
	Terrarium Plant															■			■					
Care Rating	Very Easy											■	■						■	■		■		
	Easy			■		■	■	■	■				■	■		■			■		■	■	■	
	Demanding	■	■	■		■									■								■	
	Temporary	■																						■
Other Traits	Attractive Flowers	■	■	■		■			■	■		■	■			■								■
	Climbing or Trailing				■		■	■									■				■	■		
	Colorful Foliage				■							■	■	■		■			■				■	
	Decorative Fruit																							
	Fragrance								■															

Column headers (plant botanical names with common names):

- *Radermachera sinica* (China Doll)
- *Rhapis excelsa* (Lady Palm)
- *Rhododendron* sp. (Azalea)
- *Saintpaulia ionantha* (African Violet)
- *Sansevieria trifasciata* (Snake Plant)
- *Saxifraga stolonifera* (Strawberry Begonia)
- *Schlumbergera X buckleyi* (Christmas Cactus)
- *Sedum morganianum* (Burro's Tail)
- *Senecio cruentus* (Cineraria)
- *Sinningia speciosa* (Florist's Gloxinia)
- *Solanum pseudocapsicum* (Jerusalem Cherry)
- *Soleirolia soleirolii* (Baby Tears)
- *Spathiphyllum* sp. (Peace Lily)
- *Streptocarpus hybridus* (Streptocarpus)
- *Syngonium podophyllum* (Arrowhead Vine)
- *Tillandsia* sp. (Air Plant)
- *Tolmiea menziesii* (Piggyback Plant)
- *Tradescantia* sp. (Spiderwort)
- *Zebrina pendula* (Wandering Jew)

What's in a Name?

One thing that often confuses beginning houseplant enthusiasts are plant names. At first, common names seem easier to remember, until you realize that common names are far from universal! Some plants have over half a dozen "common" names, and very different plants often share the same common name. There are at least five different "Good Luck Plants," for example. What good is a name if it can't help distinguish between two different plants?

In the "Plant Profiles" section of this book, we have listed plants first under their botanical names, a system so universal that a plant enthusiast can use the name in Japan or Poland and be fully understood. If botanical names, which are derived from Latin, look formidable at first, the more you use them, the more you will pick them up. Even beginners already know a few: If you have heard of and remember *Philodendron* or *Dieffenbachia,* learning botanical names should come easy to you. To help you learn, we have followed the botanical name with the plant's most popular common names.

INDEX